Mo

Quotable Quips...

☞   ☜

★ George Rogers, number-one NFL draft choice, on his goals for the 1984 season: "I want to gain 1,500 or 2,000 yards, whichever comes first."

★ John Feinstein, author of a book on Bobby Knight, when told that the coach had called him a "pimp" and a "whore": "I wish he'd make up his mind so I'd know how to dress."

★ Coach Mack Brown, after his Tulane football team suffered a tough loss and fell to 1-3: "I feel like the guy in the javelin competition who won the toss and elected to receive."

★ Upon meeting sportscaster Steve Albert, New Jersey Nets guard Leon Wood queried: "Are you any relation to your brother Marv?"

★ When one ump went to the mound to check out Don Sutton, long accused of doctoring the ball, he found a note in Sutton's glove: "You're getting warm, but it's not here."

FOUL
PLAYS

FOUL PLAYS

AND OTHER DUBIOUS ACHIEVEMENTS IN SPORTS

KENNETH C. DAVIS

WARNER BOOKS

A Warner Communications Company

WARNER BOOKS EDITION

Cover illustration by Terry Kovalcik
Cover design by Suzanne Noli

Warner Books, Inc.
666 Fifth Avenue
New York, N.Y. 10103

 A Warner Communications Company

Printed in the United States of America

First Printing: June, 1988

10 9 8 7 6 5 4 3 2 1

Contents

Introduction

"Games," said Benjamin Franklin, "lubricate the body and the mind."

And to think he never even saw Gaylord Perry pitch. (Don Sutton, another crafty 300-game winner, once described a meeting with Perry: "He handed me a tube of Vaseline. I thanked him and gave him a sheet of sandpaper.")

The point of this book is to remind people that sports are, after all, only games. The late sportswriter Jimmy Cannon understood this fact when he said, "Sports is the toy department of life."

It is easy to overlook that simple truth when inundated with the hype that surrounds Super Bowl Week, the World Series, the Olympics, the World Cup or, for that matter, the International Arm Wrestling Championships. During these frenzied events, a single game, a lone athletic feat, a fleeting moment of competition can be described, diagrammed and dissected in far more detail than the latest round of arms talks.

When the on-field antics of a group of overdeveloped

men and women are lauded with the reverence once reserved for the Greeks against the Trojans (no, that was *not* the first Rose Bowl game), the time has come to put some perspective back into the picture. For all the endless, pompous talk—even if we don't have Howard Cosell on Monday Night Football—about gallantry, hard work and heroics, the world of sports is able to produce an unending stream of ridiculous behavior. For instance:

★ See a daydreaming Met picked off second base during an intentional walk;

★ Watch as Garo Yepremian tries to "keek a touchdown";

★ Stay glued to your seats as college athletes "take courses" while touring Tahiti;

★ Enjoy the thrilling spectacle of a notorious quarterback dropping his pants in front of the assembled national press.

These are just a few of the thrills that await you in these pages.

In 1987, the year of the Emery Board Follies, the Corked Bat Controversy and Scab Football, *Foul Plays* is dedicated to deflating the notion that what happens on the sports page is more important than the news on the front page. Enough of touchdowns, home runs and perfect tens. This book celebrates the bizarre, unusual and sublimely ridiculous moments that truly make up the thrill of victory and the agony of defeat.

CHAPTER 1

Baseball

"Baseball was made for kids, and
grown-ups only screw it up."
—*Bob Lemon, former pitching great and
two-time Yankee manager. (Isn't everybody?)*

From Russia With Glove

By now, everybody knows that it was not, as myth has it, Abner Doubleday who invented baseball. (He must have had a great PR man, though.) It took *Izvestia*, a Soviet newspaper, to finally set us straight on the game's true origins. According to Sergei Shachin, baseball was actually invented by the Russians. As writer Shachin explains it, the Russian sport of *lapta*, an ancient game of bats and balls, was taken to California by early Russian settlers. "Baseball is the younger brother of *lapta*," writes Shachin. "This old game was taken to America ... and has now returned to us in a different form and with a strange foreign name."

(Maybe there's even an old *lapta* poem that begins, "There was no joy in Moscow...")

The sudden surge of Soviet interest in the American

national pastime was prompted by the planned inauguration of baseball as an Olympic sport in the 1992 Barcelona Games. Presumably, the Soviets are giving the game a few homegrown twists. For instance, loyal Party members will be allowed *four strikes* and will walk on *three balls*. Pitchers knocked out of a game will not be sent to the showers but to Siberia. And all Russian teams will of course be called the Reds.

Shea Forecast: Chance of Showers

During a 1986 visit to Shea Stadium, Astros fireman Dave Smith was given a wet welcome by a reliever of another sort, a Mets fan who urinated on Smith as he sat in the bullpen. Said Smith, "It's the first time I've ever been used for long relief." (When he was preparing to return to Shea for the '86 playoffs, Smith was prepared. "This time I'm going to take a raincoat.")

Hug Therapy

During his last season with the Mets, '86 World Series MVP Ray Knight earned quite a reputation for his shows of emotion. A born-again Christian, Knight liked to spread his loving feeling around the club with effusive hugs during celebratory moments. Moving to Baltimore as a free agent in 1987, Knight took his special brand of celebration with him. Not everyone appreciated it. When Knight stroked a game-winning pinch-hit single in the ninth inning of a game against Texas, he went looking for Alan Wiggins, who had scored the run and was just back from a club-ordered three-day suspension for insubordination. Wiggins, one of baseball's bad boys, was not exactly a soul mate of Knight's, but in the enthusiasm of the moment, the third baseman wanted to welcome his teammate back. Knight ran to the shortstop and gave him one of his patented hugs. Wiggins was less than thrilled, standing limply as Knight wrapped his arms around him. Said Wiggins, "It wasn't like my wife hugged me."

Weighty Matters

Down on the Fat Farm

A few years ago when he was with the Atlanta Braves, reliever Terry Forster won more attention for his waistline than his line scores, especially when late-night television host David Letterman anointed the left-handed reliever a "fat tub of goo." Wallowing in the attention his girth had brought him, Forster cut a video called "Fat Is In." Released by the Braves after the '85 season, Forster left the red clay of Georgia, tipping the scales at around 270. He pitched for California in '86, saving five and winning four, and becoming a free agent after the season.

In mid-'87, the portly Forster was signed by the Twins and sent to their Triple-A affiliate, the Portland Beavers. When he reported, the Beavers didn't have a uniform big enough to fit Forster, who was so heavy he couldn't bend down. He had to wait five days for a size 48 to be shipped from Milwaukee. Thought to weigh between 260 and 280, Forster was leaving the park one day when Beaver Manager Charlie Manuel called out, "Hey, where you guys going?"

Samurai First Baseman

One of Forster's equally rotund Atlanta teammates was Bob Horner, who gave new meaning to the phrase "heavy hitter." Horner thought that meant spending plenty of time at the buffet table. Horner's uniform size, like his salary, was fast approaching six figures. His old Braves contract had stipulated that the first baseman keep his weight under 215, but when Horner became a free agent, the Braves were looking for a cut in his pay as well as his tonnage. Horner turned up his nose at the Braves' offer, opting instead for a million-dollar bid from the Japanese.

Before inking a deal with the Yakult Swallows, Horner entertained one offer from the Charlotte O's, a Double A affiliate of Baltimore. Not only did the O's propose a monthly salary of $3,001, but several Charlotte restaurant owners tried to entice Horner with the promise of free meals to supplement the $12-a-day minor league allowance. O's owner Frances Crockett even had another plum for Horner— he could join her pro wrestling circuit. The catch was that Hulk Horner would have to keep his weight *above* 240. All these appetizers fell by the wayside when the Swallows decided they had a yen for the hefty first baseman, and he said sayonara to the American major leagues, inspiring this modern-day nursery rhyme:

> Pudgy Bob Horner
> Sat in his corner
> Hoping his contract to sign.
> The Braves wanted a cut
> So Bob stuck out his gut
> And said, "To Japan I'm a-flyin'."

Even in Japan, Horner has a fallback position. If he slumps at the plate, he can bulk up and try his hand at sumo wrestling.

Eat to Win

In discussing the approach that his hefty slugger Greg (Bull) Luzinski, generously listed at 220 pounds, used in preparing for his role as DH, onetime White Sox Manager Tony LaRussa commented, "Bull had a routine. In the first inning, he had a soda. In the second inning, he had popcorn. And in the third inning, he had a sandwich."

Chew It, Don't Eat It

While on the subject of eating, there is the story of New York Yankee reliever Steve Hamilton. A left-hander who had also played basketball for the Minneapolis Lakers, Hamilton came to the Yanks from Washington in 1963, played in two World Series and finished his career in 1972 with Chicago. His claim to fame was a headline-making pitch called the "folly floater," but he is even better remembered for the day sometime in the late sixties that he inadvertently swallowed his wad of chewing tobacco. Yankee broadcaster Phil Rizzuto later recalled, "It was the middle of the inning. He got a pitch back, kicked the dirt, then got sick. At first we didn't know what it was. Then we saw what happened. I never saw a guy get any sicker. I was on the microphone and tried to talk about something else."

Continuing this great Yankee pitching tradition, Ron Guidry once swallowed his tobacco juice, turned green on the mound and had to leave a game early. Maybe the surgeon general should add a special warning for Yankees on the sides of chewing tobacco packages: "Don't forget to spit."

Ticklish Injuries

Being the best hitter in baseball is easy. It's getting your shoes on that's tough. In 1986 Boston slugger Wade Boggs missed one start when he fell against a couch as he was pulling on his cowboy boots. That same year, Oakland catcher Mickey Tettleton was placed on the disabled list with a foot infection that may have been caused by tying his shoelaces too tight. These great baseball feats bring to mind Pat Zachry, the former pitcher who kicked the top of the dugout steps in anger after a bad inning with the Mets. The dugout won and Zachry broke his toes, disabling himself for the rest of the season. Then there's Tim Flannery. During batting practice in '87 with San Diego, Flannery drag bunted the last pitch. As he started to run, he stepped on a ball tucked beneath the tarp covering the infield. Flannery tore ligaments and was out for six weeks.

So that's what "Wide World of Sports" means when they talk about the agony of de-feet.

Job Security

Everyone knows that the toughest job in baseball is managing the Yankees for George Steinbrenner. The guy changes managers the way most of us change our socks. Unfortunately, he puts on his dirty socks—Billy Martin—

too often. Following the 1987 season, Steinbrenner had made fifteen managerial changes in fifteen seasons, including the Billy Martin merry-go-round. However, there is actually a worse job—being the Yankee pitching coach.

Through the same fourteen years, there have been twenty pitching-coach changes in the Bronx Zoo: Tim Turner, Whitey Ford, Cloyd Boyer, Bob Lemon, Boyer again, Art Fowler, Clyde King, Tom Morgan, Fowler again, Stan Williams, King again, Jerry Walker, Jeff Torborg, Williams again, King again, Sammy Ellis, Fowler a third time, Ellis again, Torborg again, Ellis again, Mark Connor, Bill Monbouquette, Ellis a fourth time and Connor again.

Apparently Steinbrenner won't rest until he finds a pitching coach who can throw a perfect game!

Steinbrenner Sucks!

G. (for Gene) Steinbrenner played three games at second base for Philadelphia in 1912. He went 2 for 9 with one RBI.

Fair or Fowl?

Baseball, as they say, is a funny game. Like the time a Portland Beavers batter hit a ball down the left field line in Tucson. As the ball headed for the corner, it hit a duck and was deflected to the left fielder, who was able to gun down the runner heading for home. One sportswriter scored the play D–7–2. Which brings to mind Dave Winfield. . . .

Birdman of Toronto

Dave Winfield and the Yankees were playing the Blue Jays during a 1983 visit to Toronto. The Blue Jays lost 3–1, but it was the sea gulls who were the real losers. Tossing warmups in the outfield between innings during a 1983 visit to Toronto, Winfield lofted a throw that hit a sea gull in midflight. The innocent bird fell dead and Winfield stood by meekly as a ball boy covered the fallen bird with a towel.

For the rest of the game, the Blue Jay fans called for tar and feathering. Winfield was relentlessly taunted by Toronto bird lovers who also pelted him with garbage. To add to his humiliation, Winfield was arrested in the dressing room after the game by Toronto police and charged with "willfully causing unnecessary cruelty to animals." Luckily Winfield was able to post bond and the charges were later dropped.

When Yankee manager Billy Martin heard reporters accuse Winfield of hitting the bird deliberately, Martin, no great Winfield fan, offered a left-handed defense: "They wouldn't say that if they could see the throws he's been making all season. It's the first time he hit the cut-off man!"

The infamous Winfield bird-murder case did not end there. In November, 1987, Canadian court officials served Winfield with a suit claiming damages of $69.16. The suit was filed on behalf of Eye Ammah Ceegull, and claimed that Winfield prevented the bird from taking flying lessons when he killed it during the game. "I'm really representing the estate of the dead seagull," said paralegal agent Bob Whyte. (A friend of Whyte's had bet him that he couldn't get the claim past court officials. Even Whyte was surprised when he did.)

More Bird Droppings

During a 1987 game at Shea, Atlanta's Dion James hit a routine fly ball off Mets pitcher Bob Ojeda. The ball struck a dove in midair, killing the bird, and dropped in for a base hit, with James going all the way to second. Two outs later, Ojeda should have been out of the inning. Instead, Dale Murphy homered to give Atlanta the lead on the way to a victory. As the '87 Mets struggled to regain their '86 form, the dead dove looked more and more like an albatross around their necks.

Birdman of Pittsburgh

Nineteen eighty-seven was a rough year for the Pittsburgh Pirates. Heading toward the bottom of the NL East once more, the Pirates knew they were in real trouble when their mascot was suspended. Free-lance artist Tom Mosser, who dresses up as the Pittsburgh Pirate Parrot, received the suspension after a flap with umpire Fred Brocklander. Just after Brocklander had made a disputed call during a Pirates loss, the Parrot rode his motor scooter onto the field and looked like he was going to throw a bucket of water on the ump. Instead he tossed a plastic ball at Brocklander. Another ump said, "If the crowd had been bigger, he could have started a riot."

His feathers ruffled, Mosser apologized, saying he was unaware that Brocklander had been involved in a controversy. "I shouldn't have done it," said the grounded

Parrot. "It was dumb." Yes, Tom. You could say it was bird-brained.

Speaking of Birds, Whatever Became of...

For one remarkable season he had the baseball world eating out of his glove. Mark "The Bird" Fidrych came up to the Detroit Tigers in 1976 and charmed all of baseball with his furious digging at the mound, talking to baseballs and handshakes for his infielders after good defensive plays. He brought a breath of fresh air to the game, and with his long, lanky frame and tousled blond hair, Fidrych was soon anointed "The Bird" for his resemblance to Big Bird of "Sesame Street." His numbers for that remarkable rookie season: 19–9, a league-leading 2.34 ERA, and four shutouts. He was Rookie of the Year. Then disaster struck. Injuries and surgery took their toll and The Bird sadly could never regain his form. Out of baseball, he cleared lots for new houses, poured cement for swimming pools and finally, ten years after The Season, he was back home in Northboro, Massachusetts, tending a small farm with pigs, cows, sheep and goats.

Next Time, Try Using a Glove

People have tried to catch baseballs dropped from some pretty strange places, like the top of the Washington Monument. But the highest drop of a baseball probably came in 1939 when Joe Sprinz, a catcher for the Pacific Coast League Seals, attempted to catch a ball dropped from a dirigible. As part of a stunt at the San Francisco World's Fair, Sprinz, who later caught for

Cleveland and St. Louis, tried to catch a ball dropped 1,200 feet from a blimp hovering above the fairgrounds.

"I had to shade my eyes," Sprinz recalled later. "I saw the ball all the way, but it looked the size of an aspirin tablet."

Sprinz probably *needed* aspirin afterward. The ball hit the hapless catcher in the mouth, and the impact cracked his jaw and knocked him out, along with five of his teeth. He did not hold on to the ball. The play was scored E-B when the blimp was charged with a throwing error.

Short People

Almost everybody has heard of Eddie Gaedel, the 3'7" midget employed by St. Louis Browns owner Bill Veeck in 1951. In his one at bat, against Detroit, the sixty-five-pound Gaedel, wearing the number ⅛, drew a walk as planned. (Gaedel died in Chicago in 1961.)

But after Gaedel, who was the shortest player in baseball? This dubious distinction probably belongs to one Frank Shannon, who at 5'2" would have towered over Gaedel. Shannon played one game at—what else— short for the 1892 Washington team and thirty-one more for the 1896 Louisville (NL) team.

Several more players checked in at the lofty height of 5'3", although most of these titans enjoyed careers that were, well, short. The roster includes outfielder Bob Emmerich, who played thirteen games for Boston in 1923; infielder–outfielder Tom Morrison, who played fourteen games for Louisville (NL) in 1895 and 1896; Yo-Yo Davalillo, brother of the more famous Vic, who played nineteen games at short for Washington in 1953;

Lou Sylvester, who played for three years between 1884 and 1887 and who also qualifies as the shortest pitcher in baseball history, having twirled six games for Cincinnati of the Union Association (he was 0–1 with one save in six appearances); and most recently, Harry Chappas, who played seventy-two games at short for the White Sox between 1979 and 1980.

The greatest short players in baseball undoubtedly were Wee Willie Keeler and Walter "Rabbit" Maranville. At 5'4", Keeler, who played from 1892 to 1910 and possessed a lifetime batting average of .345, was elected to the Hall of Fame in 1939. At 5'5" Rabbit Maranville, whose career spanned twenty-three years from 1912 to 1935, primarily at shortstop for a variety of teams, was elected to the Hall in 1954.

At the other end of the growth chart, the tallest baseball player was Johnny Gee, a 6'9" pitcher for Pittsburgh and New York (NL) from 1939 to 1946, a career basically distinguished by Gee's height. (In forty-four games, he was only 7–12 with a save.) More successful was 6'8" J. R. Richard, the Houston pitcher (1971–80), whose career ended when he suffered a stroke during his pregame warmups. There have been plenty of 6'7" pitchers, but the only nonpitcher at that height was Ron Jackson, who played first base for Chicago (AL) and Boston from 1954–60. The tallest active nonpitcher is 6'6" New York Yankee Dave Winfield.

Déjà Vu

During the 1986 season, catcher Mike Heath had RBIs off pitcher Steve Carlton pitching for three different teams: the Phillies, Giants and White Sox.

Violence in Baseball

After homering in a game in July 1985 for the only time that season, Dodger second baseman Steve Sax enthusiastically rounded the bases. As he passed third, he gave Coach Joe Amalfitano an energetic high five, breaking Amalfitano's thumb. The following April, on the occasion of Sax's next round-tripper, Amalfitano stepped back, pointed an imaginary gun at Sax and pulled the trigger.

High-Five Jive

Apart from being dangerous, high fives can be costly. Ask Lamar University's Neil Reynolds. After homering in the third inning in a game against Houston, the Cardinal first baseman rounded the bases and celebrated his clout with a high five exchanged with the on-deck batter. For this heinous act, Reynolds was called out. Because his five-fingered performance came before he crossed the plate, Reynolds had transgressed an obscure 1984 NCAA rule—intended to curtail bench-clearing celebrations—that bars contact with the runner until he has scored. Lamar's coaches argued that Reynolds should have been warned first, but even though they were right, it didn't matter. The home run was erased and Lamar lost the game 3–2.

Name Games

Worst Name in Baseball History

We all know that plenty of klutzes have played baseball. In fact, there have officially been two of them. It would be hard to imagine a worse name for an infielder than Mickey Klutts, a name that provided sportswriters with endless headline possibilities with every error. This Klutts played eight years (1976–83) for the Yankees, Oakland and Toronto. An earlier Kluttz was Clyde, a catcher who played nine years from 1942–52 with several teams.

But Klutts and Kluttz pale beside the name that must have provoked more dugout insults than any other in baseball, Ralph Pierre LaCock II, better known as Pete LaCock. Primarily a first baseman, LaCock played for Chicago (NL) and Kansas City from 1972–80. LaCock may go down in history as an answer to a Trivial Pursuit question: "Who is the son of Peter Marshall, former host of television's "Hollywood Squares"?

The best name in baseball may well belong to Urban Shocker (born Urbain Jacques Schockeor). He "electrified" the league pitching for New York and St. Louis between 1916 and 1928, leading the league in victories in 1921 and K's in '22.

Baseball's Worst Nickname

Baseball history is filled with many marvelous nicknames. Bill "Wagon Tongue" Keister. Leo "The Lip" Durocher. The Sultan of Swat. Piano Mover Smith. Pickles Gerken. Steve "Rainbow" Trout. And Doug "Eyechart" Gwodsz, so named because his last name looked like one.

But the least flattering nickname in baseball probably belonged to Michael Peter Epstein, a first baseman who played from 1966–74, including a stint with the '72

Oakland World Series champs and who was known as "Superjew." (Epstein may well be remembered best for his frustration at the legendary Gaylord Perry's unhittable spitter. After striking Epstein out once, Perry threw an assortment of pitches that looked like spitters, provoking Epstein to shout, "You cheating son of a bitch, play this game like a man.")

Team Names We'd Like to See Again

In case there is future expansion in major league baseball, the new teams might look to history when considering a name. How about bringing back the Cleveland Spiders? Or the Brooklyn Excelsiors? And a perfect choice in these condom-conscious days, the Troy Trojans!

Anybody Here Named Smith?

According to *The Baseball Encyclopedia*, there have been 117 Smiths in baseball history, far and away the most for a single surname. They include Skyrocket Smith, Klondike Smith, Broadway Aleck Smith, Phenomenal Smith, Pop Boy Smith, Riverboat Smith and four Red Smiths.

Don't Walk

Being a pitcher with the name Walker seems like asking for trouble. But there have been quite a few of them, including the Dixie Walkers, *père et fils*, along with Bill, Ed, George, Luke, Marty and Mysterious Walker. Bill Walker, who played for ten years from 1927–36, is the Walker who gave up the most—538 of them.

The All-Zoo Team

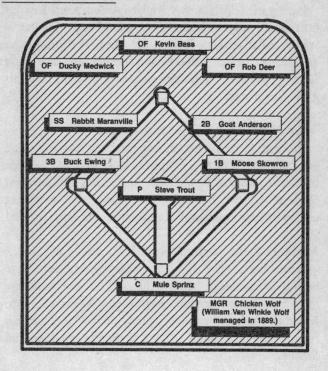

OF Kevin Bass
OF Ducky Medwick
OF Rob Deer
SS Rabbit Maranville
2B Goat Anderson
3B Buck Ewing
1B Moose Skowron
P Steve Trout
C Mule Sprinz
MGR Chicken Wolf
(William Van Winkle Wolf
managed in 1889.)

Remember the Alamo!

Davey Crockett batted .284 in twenty-eight games for Detroit in 1901.

Wheelchair Baseball

"Unless a player is really crippled, he has to be able to participate if we're going to win," said Houston Astros GM Dick Wagner in a 1986 memo to the team. (Wagner wasn't kidding. During 1987 spring training, Houston shortstop Dickie Thon, seriously injured when struck in the eye by a Mike Torres pitch several years earlier, left the camp. Thon, obviously still troubled by the incident even though his vision was medically sound, was threatened with fines by the Houston management.)

Going Down

During spring training in 1987, Baltimore O's first-year manager Cal Ripken, Sr., was riding an elevator when a stranger got on. The man was wearing only a pair of socks. "He didn't say anything and I didn't say anything," commented Ripken. "All I know is he wasn't carrying a gun." Which calls to mind New York Met Keith Hernandez. . . .

Is That a Baseball Bat, Keith? Or Are You Just Glad to See Me?

Appearing with television sex counselor Dr. Ruth Westheimer, New York Giants receiver Phil McConkey and Mets first baseman Keith Hernandez both reported that they prefer sex before games rather than after. Added Hernandez: "I'm always better to get along with when I'm on a hot streak."

X Marks the Spot

While on the subject of sex, there's the tale of Dennis "Oil Can" Boyd. We all know how boring it can get down in Florida during spring training; why, it's enough to drive a guy to extremes. Anyway, it seems the Bosox pitcher got himself into a bit of trouble during the '87 training camp when a video store claimed that Boyd owed $367 for overdue rented videotapes. The team picked up Can's tab, but a reporter who asked about the films only got some nasty words in response. An *L.A. Times* reporter turned up the reason for Boyd's touchiness on the subject. Among the film classics Boyd had kept out for so long were those cinematic marvels, *Nudes in Limbo* and *Sex Etcetera*.

With these X-ploits, Oil Can has brought a whole new meaning to the phrase, "Lets go to the videotape."

No Foreign Substances Allowed

No one can accuse Billy Martin of being shy. He speaks his mind, even if it is empty. Who can forget his comments regarding Reggie Jackson and George Steinbrenner: "One's convicted; the other's a born liar."

Then there was the time that broadcaster Martin was calling a ball game and had considerable difficulty saying the name of Red Sox shortstop Rey Quinonez. Martin had a simple, red-blooded U.S.A. solution to this linguistic problem. Have all the Latin ballplayers adopt, "American names . . . like Smith or Jones" when they make the big leagues.

Sure, Billy. And while you're at it, we can get rid of all those other funny, hard-to-pronounce names. You know—DiMaggio, Hrabosky, Hrbek, Conigliaro, Pagliarulo, Rizzuto, etc., etc.

More Clubhouse Sensitivity

Martin's comments about Latins with difficult names are lightweight when put up against Al Campanis's performance on Ted Koppel's "Nightline" early in the 1987 season. During a telecast focusing on the fortieth anniversary of Jackie Robinson's major league debut, Koppel asked Campanis, Dodger VP for player personnel and a former teammate of Robinson's, why there were no black managers, general managers or owners in the major leagues and suggested that the answer was simple prejudice. The answer left Koppel aghast and probably changed baseball history.

Campanis: No, I don't believe it's prejudice, I truly believe that they may not have some of the necessities to be, let's say, a field manager or perhaps a general manager.

Koppel: Do you really believe that?

Campanis: Well, I don't say all of them, but they certainly are short. How many quarterbacks do you have, how many pitchers do you have, that are black? . . . So it might just be, why are black men or black people not good swimmers? Because they don't have the buoyancy. . . . But they're outstanding athletes, very God-gifted, and they're wonderful people.

Campanis forgot to mention that they have great rhythm, too.

(P.S. Two days after the infamous appearance, the seventy-year-old Campanis resigned from the Dodgers following an avalanche of protest in response to his comments. Later in the year, in an extraordinary act of magnanimity, Dr. Harry Edwards, a black sociologist hired by Commissioner Peter Ueberroth to implement an affirmative action plan for baseball, hired Campanis as a consultant, citing his years of experience in baseball front offices.)

Cellar Fella

The frustration of blacks who have not been able to crack the coaching and managerial ranks is understandable in the face of the seeming old-boy network of retreads who go from one baseball helm to the next, some with the success of Captain Ahab. Take Chuck Tanner. How does the guy keep a job? With the Pirates of 1984 and '85 and the Atlanta Braves of 1986, Tanner had a three-season cellar streak going. With Atlanta picked to finish dead last again in '87, Tanner had a good shot at but missed becoming the second manager in baseball history to bottom out in four straight years, the first being Connie Mack, who did it from 1940 through 1943.

A King Among Men

Slugger Dave Kingman has a history of testy relations with the press. During his two stints with the New York Mets in the mid-seventies, he rarely spoke to reporters covering the team. Once, while with the Cubs, he dumped a ten-gallon bucket of ice water over a reporter's head. In his later years he softened, except toward women writers in the locker rooms. His disdain for lady reporters hit an all-time low in 1986 when he targeted *Sacramento Bee* reporter Susan Fornoff for special treatment. When she reported to Oakland's spring training camp, Kingman cursed at her. When he hit his 400th career homer, Kingman vowed not to speak to reporters until she left the clubhouse. The topper came when Fornoff was delivered a pink box during the 1986 season. Inside, she found a rat with a note tied to its tail, reading, ''My name is Sue.'' Fellow writers threatened to boycott the A's unless

Kingman was reined in. Oakland management later fined the unrepentant Kingman for his actions.

The Last Word on Kingman

"He's misunderstood," said sportscaster Bob Waller. "People don't have the realization of just how big a jerk he really is."

Out of Position

Playing for San Francisco in 1973, Kingman appeared as a pitcher in two games. In four innings, he allowed three hits, six walks and had an ERA of 9.00, with no decisions. He wasn't the first slugger to climb the hill to see what life is like on the other side. The "Splendid Splinter," Ted Williams, also made an appearance as a pitcher in a 1940 game, going two innings, allowing three hits and striking out one in compiling a 4.50 ERA. Fortunately Williams didn't have to make it as a pitcher. He had something to fall back on.

During the '87 season, there were an unusual number of topsy-turvy incidents with men playing out of position. In St. Louis, backup shortstop Jose Oquendo was called in to pitch the late innings of an August laugher against Philly, giving him the distinction of having played every position but catcher that year for the Cards.

In that same year, Yankee catcher Rick Cerone went out to the mound for a talk with the pitcher and found that he was talking to himself when he came on to relieve in the last inning of a 20–3 rout at the hands of the Texas Rangers. Cerone's first pitching line: one inning, no hits, no runs and a strikeout. Coming in with the bases loaded,

Cerone allowed one run to score on a grounder and then he balked in another. A foul call saved Cerone the embarrassment of a homer by Bobby Witt, a Texas pitcher (who never bats in the American League) who was brought in to pinch hit for Ranger slugger Pete Incaviglia. After his outing, Cerone said, "I didn't have my good stuff today."

Don't Quote Me

Dave Kingman knew that there were certain dangers involved in talking to the press. Just ask Texas Ranger Mickey Mahler, who didn't know any better. He told *USA Today* that if he were commissioner of baseball, he'd send every player who had played three years in the majors "back to Triple A for one month to let them see how good they have it now." The next day Mahler was sent down to Triple A.

Where Have You Gone, Pascual Perez?

We all know it's a long way from the minor leagues to the majors. Some guys never make it; others get there late. Take Pascual Perez, for instance. Called up by the Braves in 1982, Perez got lost while driving to the ball park. He circled Interstate 285 three times in search of the stadium, finally running out of gas. Borrowing money from a gas station attendant, he eventually made it to the stadium in time for the second inning.

How to Win Friends and Influence Teammates

"If you don't hustle when I'm pitching, I'll kick your ass."—Dick Bosman, ace of 1960 Washington Senators staff. On July 19, 1974, Bosman one-hit the then-champion

Oakland A's, winning 4–0. His own throwing error cost him a perfect game!

The Hot Corner

Every year it seems there is a story about some baseball fan that redefines the word and reminds us that it is short for fanatic. In San Diego, according to *Sports Illustrated*, Navy technician Ray Collins was listening to a Padres–Astros broadcast while he mowed his lawn. Collins was so intent on the game that he missed the fact that his house was on fire. By the time neighbors could alert him, it was too late for the $95,000 house. At least the Padres won 5–1.

Old Yankees Never Die, They Come Back to Pitch

At the opening of the 1987 season, the Yankee starting rotation included Rick Rhoden, age thirty-four, Joe Niekro, age forty-two, and Tommy John, age forty-four. (Both Niekro and John are older than Catfish Hunter, who was inducted into the Hall of Fame in 1987.) With two decades of baseball experience, John needed few reminders of his age, but he frequently got them when he found himself pitching against the sons of men he had played with earlier in his career. Still, none of these younger players was more disconcerting than one youngster John faced in a 1986 game. Oakland's Mark McGwire, who had two hits off John, is the son of John's dentist. As John said, "When your dentist's kid starts hitting you, it's time to go."

Whatever Became of...

Reggie bars.

Most Embarrassing Moments

★ Wrigley Field. Ninth inning. One out. The Mets have rallied to tie the score. Howard Johnson is at third with the go-ahead run. Catcher Barry Lyons is at second. After a confused squeeze play fails, Bill Almon is out at first. While the Cubs prepare to intentionally walk Mookie Wilson, catcher Jody Davis fires down to second where a daydreaming Lyons is picked off the bag, ending the Met threat. Picked off during an intentional walk!

"Lyons was looking around the park," said Met manager Davey Johnson. "That play should only work in Little League." To make matters worse, in the Cubs half of the inning, a Manny Trillo homer won it for Chicago.

★ With runners at first and third, two outs and the batting team losing 2–1, how can a game end on a single, when neither the batter or either base runner is thrown out? It happened to Atlanta in a game against Los Angeles. Glenn Hubbard was at first when Ted Simmons rapped a sharp grounder that hit Hubbard, who crumpled to the ground in pain. To add insult to the injury, Simmons was credited with a single but Hubbard was ruled out because he was hit by a batted ball and the game was over.

★ The 1987 Padres were a pathetic lot and a game against Pittsburgh early in the season seemed to symbolize all that was wrong with the team. With the score tied 5–5, Pittsburgh was batting in the seventh with runners at second and third and one out. Padres pitcher Craig Lefferts was pitching to Sid Bream, and as he went into his stretch, Bream stepped out of the batter's box. Seeing this, Lefferts stopped his motion and stepped off the rubber. The umpire, West, called a balk and Johnny Ray scored the tie-breaking run from third. West had not called time, so Lefferts should have continued his motion. The Pirates scored two more that inning en route to a 9–5 victory. Said veteran reliever Goose Gossage, "I've seen things this year that I've never seen before. It's embarrassing. It's depressing. You couldn't try to be this awful and be this awful."

Nice Work If You Can Get It

According to *Sports Illustrated*, these players are among the best paid unemployed men in America:

Steve Kemp	$1,570,000 by the Pirates
Bill Caudill	1,300,000 by the Expos
Jason Thompson	1,000,000 by the Expos and Pirates
Len Barker	900,000 by the Braves
Larry McWilliams	900,000 by the Pirates
John Castino	850,000 by Twins
Dale Berra	627,500 by the Yankees
Omar Moreno	600,000 by the Yankees
Jim Slaton	400,000 by the Angels

Aren't you glad the Pirates aren't in charge of your payroll? In addition to the hefty no-show salaries they are carrying, Pittsburgh also has to suffer the indignity of paying half of the $600,000 salary earned by Lee Mazzilli, who helped the rival Mets win the World Series in '87.

The Unkindest Cut

When you're a 29-year-old relief pitcher who hasn't won or saved many games lately, what kind of pay will you accept? For Neil Allen, that was the question, and the answer wasn't too easy to swallow. Coming off the last year of a contract that paid him $1.3 million a year, the righthander—who was 0–7 with the White Sox and 0–1 with the Yankees in '87—accepted a new Yankee contract worth about $300,000 annually. For you folks who can't subtract well, that's a million-dollar-a-year paycut. In the understatement of the decade, Allen wisely noted, "I didn't have much bargaining power."

Son, Can You Spare a Grand?

It's the American dream that sons do better than their fathers, right? Just ask Cal Ripken, Sr. Managing the Baltimore Orioles brings the senior Ripken a paltry $100,000, placing him among the league's lowest paid managers, according to a survey made in 1987 by the *Detroit Free Press*. His son, Cal Ripken, Jr., Baltimore's standout shortstop, does more than ten times better at $1,350,000 annually.

Hot and Cold Brew(ers)

At the start of the 1987 season, the Milwaukee Brewers looked like world beaters and surprised all of baseball when they opened with a string of thirteen consecutive victories, tying a major league record for the best start.

Then they did an about-face a few weeks later and looked more like egg beaters. The Brewers reeled off a string of twelve straight losses, sending them plummeting from first to third place. That prompted Brewers' rookie manager Tom Trebelhorn to comment, "Sometimes you've got to close the door and tell the guys they suck. But I never tell them that they suck until I tell myself that *I* suck. You see, the way I look at it, we suck together.''

Bill Veeck, Where Are You?

The late Veeck (as in wreck) was the first of major league owners to try promotional gimmicks to bring out the fans. What would he think of Cardinal skipper Whitey Herzog's latest idea? Herzog, aka The White Rat, suggested a new promotion in the age of AIDS—Condom Day. He even proposed an ad line—''Stretch your rubbers during the seventh inning stretch.'' The condoms, according to Herzog's overinflated idea, could be imprinted with team logos. If it works, it will bring a whole new meaning to the old baseball phrase, ''Going to the rubber.''

Sock It to Me

It's great to see that a baseball team's front office understands priorities. Take Larry Himes, general manager of the Chicago White Sox, for instance. He knew that the team he was putting on the field in 1987 wasn't going anywhere. So he wanted to make sure they looked good on the way.

Himes issued a thirty-two-page memo in spring camp outlining a revised dress code for the Sox. One point among many—the Sox must wear socks. After a 13–3 loss to Seattle, Himes found pitcher Scott Neilsen in the clubhouse, lifted his pants leg and found his feet bare inside his loafers. That cost Neilsen $100. Ivan Calderon was a two-time offender and the fine jumped to $200. At least people can say that the White Sox were one last place team that looked real good.

One-Line Drives

Bring Back Pete Gray

"It doesn't matter if his arm is sore," said Sparky Anderson about star outfielder Kirk Gibson. "He doesn't throw anyone out anyway." In 1985 Gibson had one assist in 298 chances.

Perfect Pitch

Struggling through the 1986 season, frustrated Cleveland Indians pitcher Jim Kern said, "I am working on a new pitch. It's called a strike."

How True

"It's hard to be a leader if nobody's following you." —George Foster in 1986, at the time still with the New York Mets.

Born Again

New York Mets center fielder Lenny Dykstra on former teammate Kevin Mitchell: "Mitch found God in spring training. Then every night, he'd try to find a goddess."

Speaking of Goddesses

Detroit Manager Sparky Anderson on Oakland's prize rookie of 1986, Jose Canseco: "The best thing about him, he's twenty-two and he's built like a Greek goddess."

Me and the Spitter

Languishing in the bullpen during a dull 7–0 Mets win over Pittsburgh, New York relief pitcher Randy Niemann said, "I was bored to death. I started to spit on myself to have some fun."

Speaking of Spitters

When one ump went to the mound to check out Don Sutton, long accused of doctoring the ball, he found a note in Sutton's glove: "You're getting warm, but it is not here."

Lombardozzi's Theory

The last word on the '87 season's juiced-up baseball debate goes to Steve Lombardozzi of the Twins: "They're giving steroids to the trees."

A Rose Is a Rose Is a Rose

When asked which ballplayer he'd like to be if he could be any player in history, Pete Rose said, "Me."

Dubious Achievements
(Stats They'll Never Write Home About)

Seasons of Discontent:

★ *Most Losses—Single Season Team Record*

Surprise! In 1962, their first season, the New York Mets dropped a staggering 120 decisions. Under the tutelage of the "Ole Perfesser," Casey Stengel, the Amazin' Mutts finished 60½ games behind San Francisco with a "winning" percentage of .250.

The ace of their staff was Roger Craig, now managing the San Francisco Giants and the man credited with teaching Houston ace Mike Scott and others the split-finger fastball. Craig could have used a little split-finger magic himself that season. He went 10–24 on the year with a 4.51 ERA. Craig was aided and abetted by a porous defense that led the league in errors that year with 210. Among those were the 17 committed by the Marvelous One, Marv Throneberry, which tied for the league lead for most errors at first base that year.

★ *Lowest Winning Percentage*

As bad as they were—and they were awful—the '62 Mets escaped the notorious distinction of the lowest winning percentage in baseball. That dubious honor belongs to Connie Mack's 1916 Philadelphia Athletics, whose 36–117 record amounted to a "winning" average of .235. (A year earlier, the team had gone 43–109.)

This record is all the more remarkable given the fact that the Athletics had won the Series in 1910, 1911 and 1913 while also playing in the 1914 Series.

Losses by a Pitcher

Lifetime: Among players active in 1987, **Phil Niekro** is fourth on the lifetime losers list with 274 losses, surpassing Gaylord Perry's 265 defeats and just shy of Walter Johnson's 279. In a career spanning 22 years from 1890 to 1911 with four different teams, the amazing Cy Young lost 313 games; however, they go along with his 511 all-time most victories.

Single season: In this century, the leader is **Vic Willis**, who dropped 29 games for the 1905 Boston Braves. Among the more recent big losers are two New York Mets, the previously noted **Roger Craig**, in 1962, and

Jack Fisher, in 1965, with 24 losses each. (In the good old days, Philadelphia Phillies pitcher **John Coleman** lost 48 in 1883.)

Single World Series: Reliever **George Frazier** of the Yankees would probably like to forget the 1981 fall classic against the Dodgers. His three hard-luck losses came in only 3.2 innings of relief as Frazier compiled a tidy 17.18 ERA, a performance that hardly endeared Frazier to The Boss, George Steinbrenner. (Frazier's effort tied the mark set by **Lefty Williams** of Chicago, whose defeats came in three starts during an eight-game Series in 1919.)

World Series career: **Whitey Ford.** With 8 career Series losses, the Yankee ace is the lifetime leader. However, Ford also leads in Series career victories with 10; strikeouts with 94; 22 games pitched; and 146 innings pitched.

Bases on Balls Allowed

Single season: **Bob Feller.** With 208 walks allowed in 1938, Feller holds the mark, but in that same year he made up for it by leading the league in strikeouts with 240 K's.

Single World Series: Playing for Connie Mack's Philadelphia Athletics of the American League, **Jack Coombs** put 14 runners aboard in the 1910 Series. It didn't hurt him, though, as he went 3–0 in that Series and added two more Series victories in 1911 and 1916 (for Detroit) to go undefeated in World Series play.

World Series career: **Whitey Ford.** In his eleven years of World Series experience, Ford gave up 34 free passes.

Strikeouts by a Batter

Career: **Reggie Jackson.** Through 1987, when he finally hung up his glove, Mr. October had fanned 2,597 times during his two decades on the diamond.

Single Season: **Bobby Bonds**'s 189 strikeouts while playing for San Francisco in 1970 set the standard. (The American League record belongs to **Pete Incaviglia** of the Texas Rangers, who went down on strikes 185 times in 1986, his rookie season.)

Single World Series: **Willie Wilson.** In the 1980 Series won by Philadelphia, Kansas City outfielder Wilson was fanned 12 times. He batted an anemic .154 with 3 RBIs in the six-game Series and was K'd by Tug McGraw for the final out. Wilson's World Series disappearing act was rather astonishing in light of his season statistics, when he led the league in hits, triples and runs scored while batting .326.

Fewest Hits in a Season (150-Game Minimum)

Dal Maxvill of the St. Louis Cardinals. In 1970 the former Cardinal shortstop and current St. Louis general manager piled up an astounding 80 hits in 399 at-bats over 152 games (.201 BA). Maxvill also has a share in the World Series lowest-batting-average category (minimum 15 at-bats). He went 0 for 22 in 1968 for St. Louis. Sharing the collar are **Gil Hodges** (0 for 21, Brooklyn, 1952); **Jimmy Sheckard** (0 for 21, Chicago, 1906); **Mike Epstein** (0 for 16, Oakland, 1972); **Flea Clifton** (0 for 16, Detroit, 1935).

The Black-and-Blue Heart

This award, somewhat less significant than a Purple Heart, goes to the man plunked by the most pitches. Nineteen eighty-seven saw a new champ in Don Baylor, Boston's veteran DH, who took one for the team for the 244th time in June 1987. "I can think of better ways to get my birthday present," said Baylor, who also turned thirty-eight that day. In '86, when he was hit by 35 pitches, an American League record, Baylor noted, "It's not exactly a record I stayed awake dreaming about." After he set the mark, Baylor promised a new 300 club, for those elite players who hit 300 homers and were hit by 300 pitches.

Though winning a place in the record books, Baylor can't erase the memory of the prior record holder, Ron "Pigpen" Hunt, who still holds the single-season mark of 50, as well as the one-game record of 3 HBP (in extra innings). For Hunt, a former Cardinal, Met, Dodger and Giant, being hit by pitches was something of an art that he worked on in spring training, where even the Iron Mike pitching machines hit him. As a Met in 1964, Hunt was in the All-Star game—and was hit by a pitch, a feat he repeated in the '66 All-Star game.

"I studied the rule book," Hunt later said, "and it said you have to make an attempt to get out of the way of the ball. I practiced in front of a mirror. I lined up everything right at where the corner of the plate would be, my shoulders and elbows and hips and ankles, and then twisted toward the catcher. I didn't move out of the way, but I moved. That's an attempt." Hunt finished his career wearing a rubber flak jacket inside his uniform. On the day Baylor snatched his record, Hunt was playing in an old-timers' game where, yes, he was hit by a pitch. Afterward he said, "I lead the old-timers now."

Nixon: "I Am Not a Crook"

In his twelve years of playing for Cleveland, Boston, Minnesota and Boston again, catcher **Russ Nixon** failed to steal a single base in 906 games and more than 2,500 at-bats, the major league record for futility on the base paths.

The Goats of October: Top Ten World Series Embarrassments

1912—Fred Merkle: In one of the most notorious fielding performances in World Series history, Giant first baseman Fred "Bonehead" Merkle committed three errors, including one in the decisive game seven, a ten-inning, 2–1 Boston (AL) victory over New York (NL). Another Fred, Giant outfielder **Fred Snodgrass**, shared the blame as he missed a fly to center that opened the barn door for the Red Sox to take the game and the series.

1919—Lefty Williams: One of the eight players from the Black Sox barred from baseball after the series-fixing scandal, Williams was responsible for three losses in this eight-game Series won by Cincinnati, five games to three. After pitching eight innings in both the second and fifth games, Williams surrendered four runs in the first inning of game eight.

1925—Roger Peckinpaugh: The Washington (AL) shortstop made eight of his team's nine errors as they lost a seven-game Series to Pittsburgh, which overcame a 3–1 deficit in games. In game two, Peckinpaugh's two eighth-inning errors allowed the Pirates back into a game they later won. In the final game, he made two more miscues as the Bucs won 9–7. (Peckinpaugh's eight are the all-time Series most blunders; the modern high is six by Davey Lopes in a winning cause for the Dodgers in '81.)

1927—Johnny Miljus: A walk, a bunt, a wild pitch and an intentional walk to load the bases were the undoing of Pittsburgh's "Big Serb" Miljus, a right-handed reliever. He then struck out two, including Gehrig, but next threw a wild pitch to bring home the Yanks' winning run, completing a four-game sweep by New York.

1946—Johnny Pesky: The Boston shortstop made four errors during this Series. But his worst moment came on a fielding play for which he was not charged. In the seventh game, Pesky failed to throw the ball in after a hit, allowing Enos Slaughter to score all the way from first with the deciding run, capping a 4–3 Cardinal victory.

1957–60—Tony Kubek: People forget the Yankee shortstop's two homers and 4 RBIs in 1957's game three, but remember his two errors, especially the one in game seven that allowed Milwaukee to score four unearned runs en route to a 5–0 win to take the Series. In the '60 classic, a ball struck Kubek in the neck after a bad hop, and his misplay, one of three in that Series, allowed the Pirates to score five times on the way to a 10–9 win, giving them the title.

1966—Willie Davis: The Dodger outfielder's three

successive errors—two dropped flies and a wild throw—in one inning of game two made life miserable for Sandy Koufax. Davis's .063 average (1 for 16) didn't help the Dodger cause either as the Orioles swept L.A. in four straight.

1981—George Frazier and Dave Winfield: Frazier's three-loss pitching and Winfield's .045 (1 for 22) hitting were two key reasons for the Dodgers comeback from a two-game deficit to take the Series 4–2.

1986—Bill Buckner: When the Boston Red Sox's gimpy first baseman allowed Mookie Wilson's slow roller through his legs with two outs in the last inning of game six, he also allowed the Mets to win the game and turn the tide as they went on to win game seven as well in another come-from-behind victory. (Buckner's error not only cost Boston the game and the Series but probably his job as well. In '87, with the Red Sox struggling, the veteran first baseman was released unconditionally.)

Series No-Shows

The following is a team of great players, listed with their batting averages and years of service, who never made it to the World Series, despite their long and illustrious careers:

1B George Sisler	.340	(15 years; Hall of Fame)
2B Rod Carew	.328	(19 years)
SS Ernie Banks	.274	(19 years; Hall of Fame)
3B George Kell	.306	(15 years; Hall of Fame)
OF Billy Williams	.290	(18 years)
OF Harry Heilmann	.342	(17 years; Hall of Fame)

OF Ralph Kiner   .279 (10 years; Hall of Fame)
C Rick Ferrell   .281 (18 years; Hall of Fame)
P Gaylord Perry   314 victories (22 years)
MGR Gene Mauch   1,828 victories (25 years)

Other Notable Hall of Famers Who Never Made the Series

Batters
Cap Anson 1 B   .334 (22 years)
Luke Appling SS   .310 (20 years)
Ed Delahanty OF   .345 (16 years)
Buck Ewing C   .303 (18 years)
Willie Keeler OF   .345 (19 years)
Nap Lajoie 2B   .339 (21 years)

Pitchers
Jack Chesbro   2.68 ERA (11 years)
Pud Galvin   361 wins (14 years)
Addie Joss   1.88 ERA (9 years)
Kid Nichols   360 wins (15 years)
Old Hoss Radbourn   308 wins (12 years)
Amos Rusie   243 wins (10 years)
Rube Waddell   2.16 ERA (13 years)

Most Frustrated Active Major Leaguers With No Series Experience (through 1986 Series):

Jose Cruz, Astros   2,189 games played
Toby Harrah, Rangers   2,155
Buddy Bell, Reds   2,133

Chris Speier, Cubs   2,039
Bobby Grich, Angels   2,008
Enos Cabell, Dodgers   1,688

The Niekro brothers, Phil and Joe, with a combined forty-five years and 538 wins between them, hadn't made it to the Series until Joe got there with the '87 Twins. The younger Niekro almost didn't see action, failing to get a starting nod and pitching only in relief, as the Twins went on to win the seven-game championship.

Baseball's Worst Trades

There are guys in the Rotisserie League who have never made trades as bad as the ones big league owners and general managers have inflicted on their teams and fans. One of the worst trades of the century took place in the first year of the century when the New York Giants sent one of the best pitchers in the game, future Hall of Famer **Amos Rusie**, to the Cincinnati Red Stockings for an unknown twenty-year-old prospect. Rusie, the "Hoosier Thunderbolt," had won 243 games in nine years, but he would pitch only 3 games for Cincinnati without winning in 1901. The "prospect," **Christy Mathewson**, went on to win 372 regular-season and 5 World Series games for the Giants. (A footnote to this notorious trade is that John Brush, architect of the deal, left the Reds for the Giants and so was actually working for his future team's best interest.)

If you had to pick the most lopsided and disastrous exchange in baseball history, a safe bet is the deal made on January 3, 1920, when Boston owner Harry Frazee sold **George Herman "Babe" Ruth** to Colonel Jacob Ruppert's New York Yankees for $125,000 and a $300,000 loan. Frazee liked to invest in Broadway shows and his dumping of Ruth was a quick way to raise cash for some more forgettable musicals. (The footnote to this story is the way Ruppert humiliated the aging Bambino by offering him a dollar to play the '35 season, forcing the great Ruth to leave the Yankees and return to Boston, where he played the final thirty-eight games of his glorious career for the Braves of the National League.)

A more recent Yankee steal came from Boston in 1972 when the Red Sox got first baseman **Danny Cater** for **Sparky Lyle**. A journeyman infielder, Cater played three disappointing seasons in Fenway. But Lyle saved thirty-five for the Yanks in '72 and won the Cy Young award in '77. But as Yankee teammate Graig Nettles put it, Lyle went from "Cy Young to sayonara" after the Yanks acquired free agent Goose Gossage in 1978 and Lyle was later shipped to Texas with four other players in return for five players, including a prospect named **Dave Righetti**.

New York teams have also been caught on the short side of some ghastly trades, principally involving the New York Mets. One was the 1971 trade of **Nolan Ryan** for **Jim Fregosi**. Looking to fill their black hole at third base the Mets took Fregosi, who spent one unremarkable season at third in 1972, batting .232 with fifteen errors, before being shipped to Texas forty-five games into the '73 season for cash. Ryan went on to become the all-time strike-out leader in baseball history.

The other trade that broke hearts in New York was the 1977 exchange of franchise pitcher **George Thomas**

Seaver to Cincinnati for **Pat Zachry, Doug Flynn, Steve Henderson** and **Dan Norman**, four players expected to lead the Mets into a new era that never materialized and all of whom were out of the major leagues by the time Seaver retired. That blunder was somewhat rectified in 1982 when Seaver was returned to the Mets, presumably to finish his Hall of Fame career in the place it began so gloriously. But in 1984 Mets GM Frank Cashen failed to protect Seaver in the free agent compensation draft and he was taken by the Chicago White Sox. (Following a subsequent trade to Boston, Seaver became a free agent in 1987 and was picked up for an aborted attempt at a third stint with the Mets.)

On the other hand, Mets fans could take pleasure in Cashen's engineering of a 1983 trade that must look like one of the all-time worst to Cardinals fans when the Mets obtained All-Star first bagger **Keith Hernandez** in exchange for reliever **Neil Allen**. Expected to fill Bruce Sutter's large bullpen shoes for Whitey Herzog's Cardinals, Allen rapidly self-destructed and was traded to a succession of teams, ending up with the Chicago White Sox with his million-dollar salary and an ERA almost as large. Hernandez simply continued his extraordinary level of play at first for the Mets, leading them to the championship in 1986.

The Cardinals were on the right side of an earlier trade that ranks among the best/worst in baseball history. In 1964 they gave up **Ernie Broglio, Bobby Shantz** and **Doug Clemens** for **Jack Spring, Paul Toth** and a player named **Lou Brock**. Broglio pitched poorly for two years; Shantz was soon traded to Philadelphia; Clemens was also sent to Philly. Brock simply led the Cardinals to the pennant in '64, '67 and '68 and became a Hall of Famer in 1985.

All My Bags Are Packed: The Most Traded Men in Baseball

Ten-Timers:

★ Bobo Newsom—Although he started his twenty-year career with three games for Brooklyn in 1929 and appeared in one game for Chicago (NL) in 1932, Buck Newsom's illustrious trading career began in earnest in 1935. That year he went from St. Louis (AL) to Washington. In following years, he traveled to Boston, then St. Louis again, Detroit, Washington again, Brooklyn, St. Louis again, Washington again, Philadelphia (AL), Washington again, then New York (AL). He also played for New York (NL) and later for Washington and Philadelphia. All the traveling did not help his control; Newsom's 1,732 walks are fourth on the all-time list.

★ Dick Littlefield—Between 1950 and 1958, this south-paw saw duty with Boston, Chicago (AL), St. Louis (AL), Detroit, St. Louis again, Baltimore, Pittsburgh, St. Louis again, New York (NL), Brooklyn (this trade was canceled when Jackie Robinson retired rather than be traded), Chicago (NL) and Milwaukee (NL).

Nine-timers:

★ Burleigh Grimes (1918–34)—"Ol' Stubblebeard" took in the sights in Pittsburgh; Brooklyn, New York (NL); Pittsburgh; Boston (NL); St. Louis; Chicago; St. Louis;

Pittsburgh; and New York (AL). In his nineteen years, the Hall of Famer pitched in three World Series with three different teams, Brooklyn, St. Louis and Chicago.

★ Willie Montanez (1966–82)—One of the first "hot dogs" in baseball, so called for his bat-twirling antics, he was part of the 1969 Curt Flood trade that sent him from St. Louis to Philadelphia. Then came trades to San Francisco, Atlanta, New York (NL) by way of Texas, back to Texas, San Diego, Montreal and Pittsburgh.

★ Dave Philley (1941–62)—An outfielder, he was a ten-year veteran when he went from Chicago (AL) to Philadelphia (AL), then on to Cleveland, Baltimore, Chicago (AL), Detroit, Philadelphia (NL), San Francisco, Baltimore, Houston and Boston.

CHAPTER 2

Professional Football

"This is a game for madmen."
—*Vince Lombardi*

Dubious Achievements
(Stats They'll Never Write Home About)

Worst Defeat

Almost one year to the day before Pearl Harbor, the **Washington Redskins** were hit by professional football's version of the predawn sneak attack. On December 8, 1940, the Redskins were humiliated by the Chicago Bears by a score of 73–0; to this day the most points scored in an NFL game. Papa Bear George Halas used thirty-three men in the game and fifteen of them scored as the Bears rolled up 501 yards of offense and the Bear defense converted three of eight interceptions into touchdowns. When the gun sounded to end the game, one reporter announced, "George Marshall (Washington's owner) just shot himself." The most famous quip to

43

emerge from this debacle was the Sammy Baugh answer to a question about a first-quarter dropped pass. The great Washington quarterback was asked if that dropped pass, which would have been a score to tie the game, had made any difference. Baugh's reply: "Yeah. The score would have been 73–7."

Two Inches to Glory

With the ball just inches away from the goal line, Dallas Cowboy quarterback Eddie LeBaron caught the Redskins thinking run. But instead of handing off to a plunging fullback, LeBaron dropped back into the pocket and slipped a pass to tight end Dick Bielski. LeBaron was credited with a pass of two inches, the shortest touchdown pass in history. It was one of LeBaron's few high spots of the season as the Cowboys, in their first year, went 0–11–1.

Been Down So Long It Looks Like Up to Me: The NFL's Most Sacked Quarterback

In the course of his eighteen seasons with Minnesota, the New York Giants and then Minnesota once more, scrambling **Fran Tarkenton** spent a good deal of time on his back, having been deposited on his derrière by opposing defenses on 483 occasions.

Mauled Eagle: Single-Season Sack Mark

The Philadelphia Eagles gave new meaning to the "offensive" in offensive line. Just ask the team's quarterbacks. Either that or quarterback Randall Cunningham is really a frustrated running back. Even though he was used by Eagle coach Buddy. Ryan as a "designated scrambler" in third and long situations for much of the 1986–87 season, **Randall Cunningham** still managed to set the quarterback's mark for most times sacked as he was dumped 72 times, breaking the previous record held by Ken O'Brien of the Jets. (Throw in the sack numbers for Ron Jaworski, the starter until he was kayoed with an injury, and you come up with a league record of 104 total sacks surrendered.)

Most Nauseating Sack

A quarterback will probably tell you that anytime he gets sacked it makes him sick. But there can be no doubt that the most sickening sack in recent memory was the one suffered by Washington's **Joe Theisman**. What was even more sickening was ABC's treatment of the play.

Nobody has ever accused network television of an excess of good taste. But on this play, even the most bloodthirsty football fans may have been left queasy by the sight they were served again and again. It came during a Monday Night Game in the 1985–86 season with the Redskins facing the Giants. The Giants were about to give the phrase "bone-crushing defense" a whole new meaning. Running a trick play, Theisman rolled out to his left, pursued by the fearsome **Lawrence Taylor** and Jim Burt. Taylor caught Theisman high and swung him around. There was a sickening sound and the Redskin quarterback fell limp. Taylor immediately jumped up, holding his head in fear and disgust, and frantically signaled for medical assistance for the fallen player. The impact of Taylor's tackle shattered Theisman's leg, breaking two bones and ended his season and his career.

ABC's Frank Gifford cautioned those viewers with weak stomachs not to watch the replay. His warning was well taken as ABC proceeded to show the play over and over again, in slow motion, super slow motion, and from a variety of camera angles.

Just think of the replays ABC could have shown if they had held the rights to the lions and the Christians at the Colosseum!

Super Stats
(The Worst of the Worst from the Super Bowls)

Most Interceptions Thrown

★ Individual: **Craig Morton** of the Denver Broncos threw the ball up for grabs four times in Super Bowl XII (1978, New Orleans). Playing against his former Dallas Cowboy teammates, Morton was anything but super. He completed just four of fifteen passes for 39 yards in Denver's 27–10 loss to the Cowboys.

★ Team: With **Earl Morrall** allowing three pickoffs and **Johnny Unitas** adding another, the four interceptions surrendered by the **Baltimore Colts** to the Jets in Super Bowl III (1969, Miami) set the standard. It was equaled by the aforementioned Craig Morton.

Most Fumbles

★ Individual: **Roger Staubach** of the Dallas Cowboys lost the handle three times in Super Bowl X (1976,

Miami), recovering two of them. In addition, Roger the Dodger threw up three interceptions as the Cowboys fell to the Steelers by a score of 21–17. **Franco Harris** (1975) and **Terry Bradshaw** (1979) of the Steelers both fumbled and lost the ball twice, tying for the most-fumbles-lost crown.

★ Team: **Dallas** (1978) fumbled the ball six times, recovering four of them. In 1971, **Baltimore** lost four fumbles against Dallas, a record equaled by **Denver** (1978) and **New England** (1986).

Most Turnovers

The 1978 **Denver–Dallas** game should have been renamed the **Slippery Bowl** as Denver lost the ball eight times to Dallas (four lost fumbles, four interceptions).

Most Points Allowed

The Chicago Bears didn't surprise anybody with their victory over the **New England Patriots** in Super Bowl XX (1986, New Orleans). But the 46 points they scored on an overmatched New England defense was a bit unexpected. By only scoring 10 points against the awesome Bear defense, the Patriots also won the laurels for largest margin of defeat (36 points).

Fewest Points Scored

You would think that a **Miami Dolphin** team led by Bob Griese and featuring Larry Csonka and Jim Kiick in the backfield and Paul Warfield as a receiver would be able to score some points. But the 3 points Miami put on the board with a Garo Yepremian field goal in Super

Bowl VI (1972, New Orleans) was all they would come away with that day in a 24–3 loss to the Dallas Cowboys. This was the only time in Super Bowl history that a team failed to score a touchdown. (The runner-up in this category is the **Viking** team that scored only 6 points in a 16–6 loss to the Steelers in Super Bowl IX in 1975. The Vikes sole score came on a blocked punt recovered in the end zone and a failed point-after attempt.)

The Agony of Defeat, Defeat, Defeat, Defeat

Only the few, the select make it to the Super Bowl. Just getting there is an achievement. Well, maybe. **Bud Grant** and his **Viking** teams must sure be wondering what victory champagne tastes like instead of the warm beer they have probably been served following four Super Bowl defeats. The Vikes, usually on the strength of their powerful defensive teams, made it to the championship summit four times and four times came away losers. The Vikings Super Bowl record:

Kansas City Chiefs	23—Vikings 7
	(Super Bowl IV, 1970)
Dolphins	24—Vikings 7
	(Super Bowl VIII, 1974)
Steelers	16—Vikings 6
	(Super Bowl IX, 1975)
Raiders	32—Vikings 14
	(Super Bowl XI, 1977)

(The two teams with three losses in Super Bowl play are the Cowboys and Dolphins. However, both teams have two victories to go along with their losses.)

Dumbest Pregame Comments

Prior to SB XIII (Miami, 1979), Dallas linebacker **Thomas "Hollywood" Henderson** gave the Steelers plenty of ammunition for locker room psyching. No shrinking violet (he anointed himself "Hollywood"), Henderson told the world that Steeler quarterback **Terry Bradshaw** "was so dumb he couldn't spell 'cat' if you spotted him the *c* and the *t*."

Not content with firing up Bradshaw, Henderson turned on tight end **Randy Grossman**. "Look at Grossman," said Henderson. "How much respect can you have for a backup tight end? I mean he's the guy who comes in when everybody else is dead." Henderson's words had their effect, but not the one Henderson intended. Bradshaw (17 of 30, 318 yards, four touchdowns), Grossman (three catches for 29 yards) and the rest of the Steelers had their revenge in one of the best Super Bowls of all, a 35–31 Pittsburgh victory. (In a 1987 book, *Out of Control*, Henderson revealed that he snorted cocaine through a Vicks inhaler during the second half of that Super Bowl game.)

A little too flashy for Dallas and the taste of staid head coach Tom Landry, Henderson soon afterward was in hot water. Missed practices, showboating on camera during a Cowboy loss and general un-Cowboy-like behavior cost Henderson his Cowboy job, and a later drug-related conviction cost him his career.

He's Going Back, Back, Back...

The most yards lost on a single play in the Super Bowl came in SB VI (1972, New Orleans). Dallas Cowboys defensive tackle Bob Lilly sacked Miami Dolphin quarterback **Bob Griese** 29 yards behind the line of scrimmage.

Worst Play

Bob Griese's reverse motion on that sack by Lilly was tame compared to the carnage wreaked by Griese's teammate, **Garo Yepremian**, on a play that ranks as not only the worst play in Super Bowl history but one of the all-time worst in the annals of the NFL. The "Little Tie-maker" from Cyprus, Yepremian was a steady member of the powerful Dolphin teams of the early seventies, teams that played in three successive Super Bowls (VI, VII, VIII). But it was his play in SB VII (1973, Los Angeles) that earned Yepremian his place in Super Bowl history, an unforgettably laughable moment to all the millions who saw it around the world.

There were the Dolphins, undefeated on the year, and leading the Redskins comfortably by a 14–0 score late in the fourth quarter. The Dolphins were preparing for a field goal from 42 yards out, a kick that surely would have iced the game for Don Shula's first Super Bowl victory following two earlier defeats. But Washington's Bill Brundige got a hand on the ball, which then bounced back toward Yepremian. Even though he had never thrown a pass in anger, the short, balding place kicker—who once told a reporter he wanted to "keek a touchdown"—picked up the ball, cocked his arm and looked downfield. Suddenly the ball squirted out of Yepremian's hand and he wildly, desperately batted at it in the air. Mike Bass of the Redskins picked up the wounded duck and ran it back 49 yards for Washington's only score of the day. Luckily for Yepremian, the Redskins did not score again.

Miami Coach Don Shula simply said later, "He should have fallen on it," a sentiment the place kicker later seconded. On the plane ride home, Shula was more emphatic. Calling Yepremian to his seat, the smiling Shula said, "If you ever do that again, I'll kill you."

More Worst Plays

★ The Marshall Plan

If Yepremian's misguided missile was the worst of the Super Bowl plays, another of the all-time worst NFL plays surely belongs to Minnesota Viking defender **Jim Marshall**, a stalwart member of the Vikings' "Purple People Eaters." In a 1964 game against San Francisco, Marshall picked up a 49er fumble and headed for the end zone. "I saw my teammates running down the sidelines," Marshall later said. "I thought they were cheering for me."

His 60-yard ramble resulted in a score—for San Francisco. Marshall had run into his own end zone, resulting in a safety for the 49ers. Fortunately for Marshall, the Vikings held on for a 27–22 win. (Marshall's romp recalled the most famous wrong-way run in football history: Roy Riegels's 70-yard jaunt in the 1929 Rose Bowl that made "Wrong Way Riegels" famous for life. In fact, Riegels wrote a letter to Marshall after his run, telling the Viking not to let it bother him.)

★ The Phantom Punt

Before the Giants reached their lofty summit, they had

to suffer the indignity of one more disastrous play that ranks among the pits of the NFL. Playing the Bears in Chicago during the 1986 playoffs, the Giants were holding their own against the mighty '86 Bears. The game was scoreless when **Sean Landeta** was forced to punt from deep in Giant territory. Among the league's leading punters, Landeta took his step, dropped the ball—and it kept going down. Landeta had whiffed. Chicago's Shaun Gale scopped up the ball, scampered into the end zone and the game was all Chicago from there on. Landeta later blamed it on the gusting wind. It was the first time in anyone's memory that wind shear had determined an NFL game. No wonder they call it the Windy City!

First-Round Flops
(A Collection of the Worst Draft Disasters in NFL History)

The biggest flub in NFL draft history may not have been the misguided high selection of a bad player but the shortsighted decision to drop a low pick. In 1955 the **Pittsburgh Steelers** chose six rather unmemorable players before taking a quarterback from Louisville on the ninth round. The young man was cut without playing in any Steeler exhibitions and coach Walt Kiesling told owner Art Rooney the guy couldn't remember the plays. "He's too dumb," said Kiesling. Famous last words. Going to work in a coal mine, the youngster played for a semipro team at six dollars a game when he was given a chance to play by the Baltimore Colts. The "dumb" quarterback, **Johnny Unitas**, led the Colts to three championships and became perhaps the greatest quarterback in NFL history.

When it comes to teams with daffy draft records, nobody does it like the Tampa Bay Buccaneers. In twelve years of NFL existence, the team has owned the number-one spot six times. By the end of the 1986 season, all they had to show for those premium picks was a number-five pick in the 1987 draft obtained from Washington in exchange for the rights to quarterback Doug Williams. Their luck has ranged from bad to tragic. This is the history of Tampa's number-one picks:

1976: Lee Roy Selmon, DE. Perhaps the best of the Bucs, he played in six Pro Bowls but retired in 1984 after nine seasons.

1977: Ricky Bell, RB. Traded to San Diego in 1982, Bell played five season, but died in 1984 of a muscular disease.

1978: Pick traded to Houston for four picks, one of which was used to draft Doug Williams. Houston used the pick to acquire Earl Campbell.

1984: Pick traded to Cincinnati; in return received Jack Thompson, a quarterback known as the "Throwin' Samoan," who played part-time for two seasons at Tampa. Cincinnati in turn gave the pick to New England, who used it to acquire Irving Fryar, the explosive receiver and kick returner.

1986: Bo Jackson, RB. Spurning the lucrative offer Tampa placed before him, the Heisman winner from Auburn chose to play baseball instead, signing a major league contract with Kansas City. After a season in the minors,

Jackson got off to a hot start in 1987, only to slow down in all departments except striking out. Given his epic strikeout ratio, Jackson decided on an unusual "hobby." He anounced in midseason his signing of a contract with the L.A. Raiders and said he would attempt to play both sports, moving from the outfield to the backfield once the baseball season was over. Kansas City fans and team-mates were not thrilled with this announced "hobby," and it remains to be seen if Bo can go both ways.

A footnote to Bo Jackson's two-sport decision is the proposal that came from Tim Leiweke, president of the Kansas City Comets of the Major Indoor Soccer League. Leiweke has offered Jackson a contract. After all, Bo will have three whole weeks between the end of football season and the opening of spring training; the guy will need something to keep him busy. Said Leiweke, with his tongue firmly planted in his cheek, "It's a good hobby for three weeks. Anybody with that much athletic ability we'll use in goal."

There's only one condition to go with the offer: Bo will have a contract clause that won't let him play in the NBA!

1987: Vinny Testaverde, QB. Beware the Curse of Tampa, Vinny!

Broken Record

With that draft track record, it is small wonder that the Bucs have had the NFL's worst record since they came into existence. Since 1976, when they went 0–14, the first team to go winless since the 1960 Dallas Cowboys, the Bucs have compiled a 49–104 record. They have made the playoffs three times in that stretch, twice as Central Division Champions, once as a wild-card team, and are 1–2 in the playoffs. They finished 2–14 in both 1985 and 1986. Leeman Bennett, the coach during those two seasons, was sacked at the close of the 1986 campaign, which brings to mind . . .

The Jimmy Carter "I'll Never Lie to You" Award

To Ray Perkins, named head coach of the Tampa Bay Buccaneers in 1987. In 1979 Perkins came to the New York Giants and was given much credit for helping to turn the team around from its disastrous state. He also signed a contract that would have assured his presence with the Giants for some years to come. But lured by his alma mater, Alabama, where Bear Bryant was retiring, Perkins broke his contract with the Giants, announcing his departure at the end of the season when the Giants were still in a position to make the playoffs. Deflated by Perkins's leaving, the Giants stumbled through the rest of the season and finished out of the running. At Alabama, Perkins said he had the job he always wanted and would never leave. Until, that is, Hugh Culverhouse, owner of the Tampa franchise, lured Perkins farther south. Las Vegas is planning to set up a betting line on how long Perkins will stay at his latest "only job I ever wanted."

Worst Trades

A record-setting quarterback at LSU, **Y. A. Tittle** was drafted by the Detroit Lions of the NFL but signed instead with Baltimore of the now-defunct All-American Football Conference in 1948. When that team folded in

1950, Tittle's NFL rights were taken by San Francisco and the balding quarterback played with the 49ers for ten years. With the arrival of John Brodie, San Francisco thought Tittle was expendable and sent him to the New York Giants. In the years after the trade, Tittle simply led the Giants to three NFL Championship games in four years. In 1962 he also set an NFL record with thirty-three touchdown passes, then broke it the next year with thirty-six.

In return for Tittle, the 49ers received journeyman guard **Lou Cordileone**, no doubt making for one of the greatest talent heists in NFL and perhaps all sports history. Even Cordileone knew something was rotten. Upon learning he had been traded even up for Tittle, Cordileone commented: "Me for Tittle? Just me? Who else?" Tittle, when he heard he had been traded for Cordileone, simply said, "Who?"

1964 was a year of strange trades, chief among them a quarterback switch that in hindsight leaves you scratching your head. Sonny Jurgensen joined the Philadelphia Eagles in 1957, a fourth-round choice out of Duke, and he played backup to Norm Van Brocklin. After seven seasons with the Eagles, including a record-setting 1961 campaign, Jurgensen was shipped to Washington for Norm Snead, who had been Washington's number-one pick in 1961 out of Wake Forest. Needless to say, Washington got the better of the deal; Jurgensen, one of the game's great pure passers, led the NFL in passing twice and the NFC once. He was inducted into the Hall of Fame in 1983. Snead, a competent but uninspired quarterback, stayed with Philadelphia for a few seasons before bouncing around to a variety of teams, none of which was very memorable or successful.

The other strange trade of that 1964 season was the Giants decision to unload the anchor of their great defense of the era, linebacker Sam Huff, prototype for NFL middle linebackers for years to come. The departure of Huff, admittedly near the end of his career, signaled the beginning of the demise of the Giants as a force in the NFL.

Key Date in American History

November 1963: During the Army–Navy game, after Army's Rollie Stichweh ran for a touchdown, CBS viewers were shown the play again. It was the first instant replay in football history, the creation of CBS director Tony Verna.

The Art and Science of Choosing a Coach

After being fired by the New England Patriots eight games into the 1984 season, Ron Meyer was called "the sorriest excuse for a football coach I've ever seen," by All-Pro John Hannah. (One year after Meyer's dismissal, Ray Berry took the Pats to the Super Bowl in 1986. Unfortunately, the Chicago Bears were also there.)

In spite of this ringing recommendation by one of the most respected players in the game, Meyer nevertheless rebounded by being hired by the Indianapolis Colts, one of the NFL's sorriest franchises. Colts General Manager Jim Irsay, twenty-seven-year-old son of owner Robert Irsay, commented on the Meyer hiring: "The New England thing was a good experience for him." (See Robert Irsay under "Foul Plays Hall of Fame.")

More Art and Science: Maybe It's Our Breath?

"Wanted: Head Coach. Successful Experience Not Required." Following another season of mediocrity in 1986, the Atlanta Falcons sacked head coach Dan Henning. Owners Rankin and Taylor Smith then began the search for a successor. Dick Vermeil wasn't interested. Neither was Terry Donahue of UCLA. Also giving the thumbs down in rapid succession were Bill Parcells of the Giants, Chicago's Mike Ditka and Denver's Dan Reeves. Cars in Atlanta were soon sporting this bumper sticker: "Honk if you've turned down the Falcons." (In a stroke of owners' genius, the Smiths turned to assistant coach Marion Campbell, who had previously been the team's head coach and had been fired after five games in 1976.)

Press Restrictions

Certain that the press had been responsible for all of the derisive laughter aimed in their direction over the coaching-choice fiasco, Atlanta's Smiths decided to take action. The Falcons declared the office bathrooms at their Suwanee, Georgia, training camp off limits to the press. Reporters who feel the need must now walk a block to a nearby hotel. To underscore their feelings about the fourth estate, the Smiths also had a wall built within the training complex that cut off the press room from access to the rest of the offices. And just to make sure everyone got the point, press relations director Charlie Dayton was fired. Spiro Agnew would be proud of the Smith family.

Van Brocklin Gets Last Laugh

The late Norm Van Brocklin, a Hall of Fame NFL

quarterback and later a rather fiery head coach with the Vikings (1961–66) and Falcons (1968–74), had a love–hate relationship with the press. The press loved to goad Van Brocklin and he hated the press in return. Following his 1980 brain surgery, Van Brocklin got in last licks at the press world in discussing his operation: "It was a brain transplant. I got a sportswriter's brain so I could be sure I had one that hadn't been used."

Eternal Optimist

With his team trailing 42–0 in a 1967 preseason game against Kansas City, Oakland defensive tackle Dan Birdwell joined a fourth quarter huddle and told his teammates: "Come on, guys, let's hold 'em. If we get seven quick scores, we've got 'em beat."

The Long and Short of It

The flea flicker can be a very useful weapon in the football arsenal. But that doesn't mean you need to keep a lot of fleas on the roster. Houston Oiler coach Jerry Glanville knew his quarterbacks needed somebody a little taller to throw to as he went into the 1987 NFL draft; his incumbent receivers, Drew Hill and Ernest Givins, both stood at 5'9"—not big enough by current NFL standards. In the first round, the Oilers went for 6'2" Haywood Jeffries out of North Carolina State. After taking Jeffries, Glanville said: "We wanted a receiver who couldn't qualify as a jockey."

Name Games

★★ *Best Names In Football*

There's a toss-up here between Jarvis Redwine, the former running back and kick returner for Minnesota, and former Rams–Cincinnati running back Elvis Peacock with the judge's decision going to Peacock because his name has more color. As Elvis said himself: "I like my name. Not too many people have it." (Not exactly, Elvis, but there was a Johnny Peacock who played defensive back for Houston in 1969–70.)

★★ *Now Say It Three Times Fast.*

The entertaining Bob Costas of NBC is a witty broadcaster who doesn't take himself too seriously. Calling a 1980 New England–Seattle game, Costas reached a moment that would have made other broadcasters cringe. "Don't fix your sets," said Costas, "I've been waiting for this all day. Mosi Tatupu runs into the arms of Manu Tuiasosopo."

Shirt Tales

You know those annoying T-shirts that say something like, "My parents went to Florida and all I got was this dumb T-shirt"? Well, pass one over to retired Atlanta Falcons center Jeff Van Note. Van Note, who hung up his jock after the 1985–86 season at age forty, was miffed at his former teammate Bill Fralic, and called him a "cheap son of a gun" after Fralic returned from his Pro Bowl trip with ordinary T-shirts for his offensive line colleagues. It seems that Van Note had begun a tradition of bringing back *genuine* Hawaiian shirts during his Pro Bowl trips and expected any Falcon Pro Bowler to do the same.

Unfazed by the criticism, Fralic said, "I didn't even figure Van Note would care. I figured that by the time I got back from Hawaii, Note would be dead of old age."

The Fall Line From Wisconsin

Speaking of shirts, after being waived by the Green Bay Packers in 1986 and later being claimed by Miami, Greg Koch commented, "When people in Green Bay say they have a nice wardrobe, it means they have ten bowling shirts."

Green Bay Attackers

Maybe it's all that cold weather and cabin fever, but Green Bay does seem to make some people do some strange things. For instance, while the Packers faltered through another disappointing year during the 1986–87 season, they did lead the league in one dubious offensive category: sex offenses. In unrelated incidents, two Packers, receiver James Lofton and defensive back Mossy Cade, were arrested for sexual assault. Cade was found guilty in 1987 and Lofton was acquitted. The constitutional presumption of innocence was no protection in Lofton's case, as the Packers shipped him off to the Los Angeles Raiders before he was even tried.

There Is No There There

There are plenty of Green Bay boosters who might disagree, but after all, it is a one-reindeer town. Wide receiver John Jefferson, traded from San Diego to Green Bay in 1981, had this reaction as his airplane approached his new home in the NFL's winter wonderland: "I was wondering why we were stopping. I didn't see any lights down there and I was starting to get a little worried.''

Packing It Away

It worked for William Perry; why not for Donnie Humphrey? At some point in his career, Humphrey, a defensive lineman for the Packers, was probably told to bulk himself up. The problem is, nobody told him when to stop. The former Auburn player started sixteen games for the Pack in 1984, then developed weight problems following a month in a cocaine rehabilitation program. During the 1986 season, he weighed around 295 pounds, but Coach Forrest Gregg wanted his burly defenseman to play at closer to 270. When Humphrey reported to a 1987 preseason camp, he literally tipped the scales at 335 pounds, 65 pounds above his ideal playing weight. Already a dropout from one nutritional program, Humphrey was sacked by the Pack.

Tubby the Tuba Strikes Back

A happier fat story is the saga of Chuck Rogers, who did not play football while in high school or college at the University of Dayton. He did, however, play the tuba in the school's marching band. That did not prevent the San Diego Chargers from signing the 6'9", 360-pounder to a contract in 1987. Said Ron Nay, Chargers director of scouting, "If he makes it, he'll set scouting back ten years." (The system was safe for another year as Rogers was cut after the first few sessions of summer camp.)

More Weighty Matters

Mike Ditka, Chicago Bears coach, on William Perry after 1986 summer camp: "He worked out religiously until a week ago, and then he went home to South Carolina. That's usually a catastrophe. The chicken population of South Carolina goes down measurably."

William Perry on William Perry. In London for a 1986 exhibition against Dallas, a youngster wanted to take a photo with the Fridge to "make a lot of money," and Perry responded, "Nowadays all kids think about is money. When I was a kid all I thought about was eatin'."

Higher Math

Maybe keeping tabs on William Perry and Jim McMahon has jangled Mike Ditka's head for numbers. Anyway, this was his assessment of the 1986 midseason acquisition Doug Flutie, who had considerable problems with changing plays at the line of scrimmage: "He'd call our audibles half the time, Boston College's half the time and New Jersey's half the time." But who's counting. Right, Mike?

Three Strikes and You're Out

Speaking of weird counting, there was the time that Norm Schachter forgot how to add. As the one-time NFL ref described it in his book *Close Calls*, at the end of a 1968 Rams–Bears game, the Rams had the ball and were driving for a field goal that would win the game. A holding penalty took the ball out of range, but with the down repeated, L.A. quarterback Roman Gabriel still had three shots left to position a fourth-down kick. Right?

Apparently not. After three Gabriel passes fell incomplete, Schachter and his crew gave the ball back to the Bears. The Rams had been robbed of their fourth down. Nobody noticed until it was too late; the game was over and decided. The Bears laughed. The Rams cried. And the refs paid fines. They were also kept out of any postseason contests as punishment for their lower math.

Say What, George?

In 1980 it was obvious that George Rogers had won the Heisman Trophy and not the Rhodes Scholarship. While playing for the New Orleans Saints, the number-one draft choice was asked about his goals for the 1984 season: "I want to gain 1,500 or 2,000 yards, whichever comes first."

Money Isn't Everything, It's the Only Thing

You would think that with NFL salaries averaging well over six figures, players wouldn't have to resort to larceny to get by. Not so, according to the *Dallas Morning News*, which reported in 1987 that scalping of Super Bowl tickets by players was commonplace. Allowed to buy two tickets at face value of $75, many players were reselling their tickets at huge profits, said the newspaper. A former Pro Bowler told a reporter that it was easy to turn ten tickets into $4,000. "You're looking at a clear profit. It's hard to turn down. It's so tempting your mouth waters," he said. "If you don't need them for youself, you say, 'Heck, I'm selling these babies.' It's such easy cash money, and Uncle Sam doesn't get any of it." One player sold two tickets to the

Giants–Denver game in Pasadena for $1,600, a profit of $1,450. At this rate, the players' union may forget the free agency issue and simply demand more freebies!

Place Your Bets

The notion of well-paid players scalping tickets is bad enough. Picking up pocket money on the odd wager is a totally different thing. Paul Hornung and Alex Karras found out exactly how different an offense it was back in 1963. Hornung, the bad boy of the dominating Green Bay Packers teams of the early sixties, was called into Pete Rozelle's office during a gambling investigation by the league and eventually admitted he had placed bets on Green Bay games during the previous four years. Rozelle suspended him for a year. Hornung later wrote in his autobiography, "I think there were two reasons I started to bet. One, just for pure kicks. Two, when it looked like I might make the Pro Bowl, I wanted to have some walking around money on the coast."

Alex Karras of the Detroit Lions told an interviewer that he bet on games too. "Who doesn't?" asked Karras. Pete Rozelle for one. Even though Karras tried to cover his bets by saying he only meant he wagered things like cigarettes, the commissioner didn't go for the story and Karras, like Hornung, had to sit a year.

Great Moments in Broadcasting

The silver-tongued Howard Cosell, covering the Redskins on ABC's Monday Night, Football, on slippery Washington back Alvin Garrett: "That little monkey gets loose, doesn't he?" Some viewers and ABC execs were not amused at the reference to Garrett, who is black. Cosell haters everywhere got to enjoy the spectacle of Mr. Tell It Like It Is eating his words. Given his flatulent vocabulary, it must have made quite a meal. (For more about Cosell, see "Foul Plays Hall of Fame.")

The Wiffle Bowl

Remember the World Football League? Really stands out, doesn't it? This bogus league got started in 1973 when twelve teams were fielded along with some new rules and a "Dickerrod," a device that supplanted good old first-down chains. Among the memorable teams: the Philadelphia Bell, Chicago Fire, the Hawaiians, and the Shreveport Steamers. Dubious from the start, the WFL was taken seriously when some well-heeled owners began shelling out major league bucks to lure established NFL stars away, including Csonka, Kiick and Warfield, three main ingredients in Miami's success.

But the first World Bowl, played in Birmingham, Alabama, indicated the troubles the league faced. The Birmingham Americans had missed five payrolls; their opponents, the Florida Blazers, fifteen. Players from both teams threatened to boycott the game. Florida was the sentimental favorite to win, as *Sports Illustrated* put it, "because of greater deprivation." Coach Jack Pardee and his coaches were providing the toilet paper for the locker room. The Americans held on for a tight 22–21 victory and when it was over a Florida player dashed off with the ball, but Birmingham players caught him under the stands and recaptured their game ball. After the game, sheriff's deputies repossessed the Americans' uniforms to be sold later by a local sporting goods store.

The WFL died a merciful death in 1975, halfway through its second season.

Scab-Ball: Tales of the UN–FL

The Counterfeit Bills. The Miami Weakfish. The New York—ants. The Indianapolis Dolts. As football goes, these so-called replacement teams didn't go very well at all. And as strikes go, the 1987 NFL players strike was pretty disastrous on all counts: rookies, rejects and grocery clerks in the guise of NFL professionals, and the owners and networks trying very hard to pass it off as the real thing. Of course, the fans were the big losers, but we did manage to get a few laughs out of it too.

Coffee and...

While some strikebreakers were greeted with eggs and unloaded shotguns, it was a different story in Pittsburgh. In this tough town where unions are pretty sacred, scabs were subjected to a new horror—the players they were replacing bombarded the strike breakers with jelly doughnuts. And they weren't even stale.

And It Was a Nice Sunday for a Drive Too

When fans stayed away in droves from the scab games, owners did their best to put a happy face on things. The most pathetic alibi award went to Vikings GM Mike Lynn who produced this novel explanation for the turnout of 13,911: "Opening week of duck-hunting season is traditionally our biggest no-show week."

Sad Sack

The biggest individual loser in the strike may have been Jets defensive end Mark Gastineau, inventor of the now outlawed sack dance. Gastineau already had few friends among his teammates when he decided to cross the picket line from day one of the strike. His reward: spit on his car from a teammate. Gastineau claimed he had to cross to meet his alimony payments. That was news to his ex-wife who said she hadn't seen any of his $775,00 salary in months. Unable to produce a sack in the '87 preseason or in either of the first two regular games, Gastineau was taking a lot of heat for failing at his one-time specialty. Much of the heat came from other Jets. When Gastineau still didn't reach the quarterback in the first scab game, the mocking rose to new heights. Jet tight end Rocky Klever and two teammates went to a bar to watch part of the next scab game. Said Klever: "We were going to chug a beer every time Mark got a sack, but by the end of the first quarter, we were kinda thirsty. So we said we'd chug a beer every time he made a tackle, but by halftime we were *really* thirsty. So then we just said we'd chug a beer every time he lined up."

CHAPTER 3

School and College Football

"Football today is a social obsession. Football is a boy-killing, education-prostituting, gladiatorial sport. . . . I do not know what should take its place, but the new game should not require the services of a physician, the maintenance of a hospital, and the celebration of funerals."
—Shailer Mathews, Chicago Divinity School dean, on football in the late nineteenth century.

As they say, the more things change, the more they stay the same.

Dubious Achievements

Heisman-Schmeisman

It seems only natural that the winner of the Heisman Trophy, awarded to (supposedly) the most outstanding college football player in the land, is an automatic high draft choice and a guaranteed success in the pros. Right? Let's check the record of a few recent Heisman winners and how they stack up against other players drafted in the same year. Then think about it. Who would you rather have on your NFL franchise?

1985: **Bo Jackson**, running back. Signed by Tampa Bay, Jackson opted for a baseball contract with Kansas City (see "First Round Flops" in Pro Football chapter). If they had bypassed Jackson, who had stated a preference for baseball, the sorry Buccaneers might have selected nose tackle Tony Casillas, who went second in the draft to Atlanta; Jim Everett, the Purdue quarterback taken by Houston and traded to L.A. where he starts; Reuben Mayes, the rookie running sensation with New Orleans; or future defensive standouts Eric Dorsey, Mark Collins and Pepper Johnson, all chosen by the Giants. Whether Jackson plays two sports or opts for one, the big loser is Tampa Bay.

1984: **Doug Flutie**, quarterback. Signed by Donald Trump and the USFL's Generals, Flutie was not selected until the NFL draft's eleventh round by L.A. His rights were later traded to Chicago, where he started several games in 1986 with mixed results. Who else was drafted that year? How about Bill Fralic, All-Pro for Atlanta; Mark Bavaro, super tight end for the Giants; or the two prototype wide receivers of the 1980s, Al Toon of the Jets and San Francisco's Jerry Rice.

1983: **Mike Rozier**, running back. Signed by the Pittsburgh Maulers of the USFL, Rozier was later taken by Houston in a supplemental draft of USFL players.

Had he been available, Rozier certainly would have been a high pick. Or you might think about Jay Schroeder, selected eighty-third overall by the Redskins; Louis Lipps, Pittsburgh's game-breaking receiver; or standout linebackers Carl Banks of the Giants and Wilber Marshall of Chicago.

1982: **Herschel Walker**, running back. Walker dropped out of college to join the USFL Generals with a year of eligibility left. Undraftable that year by the NFL, Walker certainly would have been one of the top picks in the 1984 draft. The runners-up to Walker were John Elway and Eric Dickerson, who went 1 and 2 in the '83 senior draft. Others available that year—the year of the quarterback—were Todd Blackledge, Tony Eason, Ken O'Brien and Dan Marino, as well as running back Kurt Warner, taken by Seattle, and All-Pro defensive back Terry Kinard of the Giants.

1981: **Marcus Allen**, running back. This is a case in which a lot of pro scouts had to eat crow. Eight teams had a shot at Allen, who has become one of the league's premier backs. Some of the players taken prior to Allen make some sense: Jim McMahon (number five), Gerald Riggs (number nine), and Chip Banks (number three). Others are more difficult to fathom as going before Allen. Guard Mike Munchak was taken by Houston (number eight); Darrin Nelson, a running back taken by the Vikings (number seven); and the real losers, Baltimore, with two first-round choices, took linebacker Johnny Cooks (number two) and quarterback Art Schlichter (number four).

* * *

Dipping back a little deeper into Heisman history, you can find such winners as: **Archie Griffin**, the only two-time winner (1974–75), who was drafted twenty-fourth in 1976 in the same class as Giant Harry Carson, Raider Mike Haynes, back Mike Pruitt and tight end Dave Logan; **John Cappelletti** (1973), who was taken eleventh by the Rams and had a long but unspectacular career. Some of the others in his class include: future Hall of Fame defensive ends John Dutton and Ed "Too Tall" Jones, quarterback Danny White, Oakland's great tight end Dave Casper and three Pittsburgh heroes, Lynn Swann, Jack Lambert and John Stallworth.

Bye-Bye, Bernie

Bernie Kosar is miffed. And it's understandable. The young Cleveland quarterback had a splendid collegiate career, leading the Hurricanes of Miami to a dramatic 31–30 Orange Bowl victory over Nebraska in 1984, clinching the Hurricanes' number one ranking that year. Kosar was also the "other" quarterback in one of the most amazing collegiate aerial battles ever, the 1984 "Hail Mary" game between Miami and Boston College. That game, called one of the greatest collegiate contests ever, ended with Doug Flutie's extraordinary 64-yard scoring pass with six seconds on the clock. Often overlooked are Kosar's numbers for that game: 25 of 38 for 447 yards and 3 TDs; he also hit eleven straight passes to open the second half.

But when it came time to retire a quarterback's jersey down at the alma mater, it was Kosar's successor, Vinny Testaverde, who was granted the honor. It was only the third number so honored in Miami grid history. Kosar argued that his statistics were equal to Testaverde's and that he had brought the school bowl victories and a national title. While Testaverde had won the Heisman, he was 0–2 in bowl action and the team had missed the national championship under his direction.

But there is most likely another reason that Kosar was spurned. Opting for the NFL's supplemental draft in 1985, in which he was assured of going to hometown Cleveland, Kosar had passed on a year's eligibility. For that act of perceived disloyalty, Kosar's number will have to wait for retirement.

The Longest Run

Just about everyone has heard of **Roy "Wrong Way" Riegels**, the California lineman whose name went down in sports history for his singular play in the 1929 Rose Bowl. Gathering up a Georgia Tech fumble, he set off for the end zone. As 66,000 fans watched, Riegels rumbled toward a score. For Georgia Tech! Riegels actually ran into the wrong end zone but was pulled back by a teammate. On the next play California tried to punt out of danger, but it was blocked for a safety, providing Georgia Tech with the 8–7 margin of victory.

A longer but less famous wrong-way run was the ramble of **Raymond "Snooks" Dowd** of Lehigh. In a 1918 contest, Snooks ran the length of the field for an apparent touchdown, realized he was in his own end zone, rounded the goal posts and scampered back another 100 yards for a real touchdown—a scoring run of 210 yards. History fails to show where the defense was during his lengthy scramble.

The Longest Day

63	63	54	42
0	0	0	0

Those were the quarter-by-quarter scores in the most one-sided game in college history. The Yellow Jackets of **Georgia Tech** manhandled, mauled, squashed, devastated and totally demoralized **Cumberland College** with a 220–0 victory that took place on October 7, 1916. Cumberland allowed thirty-two touchdowns and 968 yards. Thirteen of Georgia's scores came on turnovers and special teams plays. It was actually a game that never should have been played, as Cumberland was a small school with a pick-up squad and Tech was a major national collegiate power coached by John Heisman. (Yes, that Heisman.) On the first play from scrimmage, the Cumberland quarterback was knocked out of the game and carried away by stretcher. His teammates should have been so lucky.

With a 126–0 halftime lead, Coach Heisman, in the true spirit of college sportsmanship, told his men, "We're in front, but you never know what they have up their sleeves." In retrospect, you might wonder if they even had arms up their sleeves.

Real Men Don't Substitute

Coach Heisman had a reputation as a bit of a martinet who ran up scores for the benefit of the writers who voted on the national collegiate football rankings. He was also a true pioneer, responsible for major developments in the game. In fact, he played for Brown and Penn from 1887–91 when the game was in its earliest evolution, and he once recalled those dinosaur days. "Players of my time had to be real iron men, because we played two games each week. Once a game started, a player could not leave unless he actually was hurt, or at least, pleaded injury. Whenever the captain wanted to put a fresh player into action, he whispered, 'Get your arm hurt.' In one game, my captain told me, 'Heisman, get your neck broke.'"

Real Men Don't Wash, Either

Bringing this Spartan attitude to his coaching philosophy, **Heisman** ordered some strange prohibitions during training. For instance, he would not allow his players to take hot water baths or use soap during the week because they were, in his words, "debilitating." This gave birth to the B-O Defense, feared by all in its day.

Sean Landeta Award for Worst Punt

To **Jay Kelley** of Santa Clara. During a game in the Roaring Twenties, undermatched Santa Clara had battled the favored Golden Bears of California into a scoreless game late in the fourth quarter. In an attempt to bury California deep inside its own territory, Santa Clara called on Kelley to punt. The kick sailed almost straight up, arced backward to land behind Kelley and then rolled the wrong way. California got the ball on Santa Clara's 37-yard line and quickly scored the winning touchdown. Kelley was credited with a punt of 25 yards. It is not known if Kelley was awarded the game ball by a grateful Golden Bears team.

Toothless Lions: The Longest Losing Streak

Records, we are told, are made to be broken. But there are some records that teams would be just as happy not to possess. No doubt the Wildcats of Northwestern are breathing easier these days. From 1976 to the midpoint of the 1982 season, the boys of Northwestern set the longest losing streak in major college grid history, a schneid that reached 34 consecutive defeats until the Wildcats toppled that football powerhouse, the Northern Illinois Huskies, by a score of 31–6.

After that, the fans of Northwestern could only sit and hope for somebody to come along and erase their shame. Help finally came in the form of a football team from Columbia University, proud member of the Ivy League. In October, 1987, Columbia "won" the dreary distinction following a 38–8 drubbing at the hands of Princeton. At the game, one nine-year-old boy carried a sign, "Please win before I grow up." As the season went by and the Lions fell to 0–7, extending their winless streak to 38 games, they closed in on the all-time college record of 50 straight losses set by the Macalester Scouts, a Division III school, between 1974 and 1980. With one game remaining in the 1987 season, Columbia had reached the 40-loss mark with a 31–20 loss to Cornell. That came a week after the Lions' nearest miss: a 35-yard winning field goal attempt hooked left and missed by a yard in the waning seconds of a game against Dartmouth.

One diplomatic opposing coach said, "It's only a matter of time before Columbia starts winning football games." Of course, that's also what Napoleon's generals told him about the war in Russia.

The High Cost of Victory

New York's Iona College was working on a streak of its own in '87 as the Gaels dropped 27 straight. But with a 27–0 victory over St. Peter's, the team was ready to celebrate. Some of the players decided a Gatorade dousing—a la Bill Parcells—was in order, and the Iona coach got wet. In the ensuing excitement, one of the players who had hoisted the Gatorade bucket jumped up for a high-five, came down and twisted a knee, knocking himself out of action for several weeks. So much for the joy of victory.

Bring on Columbia

After Oklahoma demolished UCLA by a score of 38–3, Sooner coach Barry Switzer told his team, "We were too big and strong for UCLA. That won't be the case against Minnesota." The warning must have sunk in. Oklahoma beat Minnesota 63–0.

That's One Way to Put It, Coach

Commenting on that same 38–3 drubbing of his Bruins at the hands of the Sooners, UCLA coach Terry Donahue commented, "We had some real weaknesses exposed in our program." You can say that again, Terry.

Key Date in American History

1876: During the Yale–Princeton game, legend has it that the first forward pass in football history was thrown. Yale's Walter Camp, when tackled, threw the ball forward to Oliver Thompson, who went in for a touchdown. Princeton claimed a foul and protested. The referee tossed a coin to make his decision and allowed the touchdown. Just imagine, if it had been heads instead of tails, Joe Namath and Jim McMahon would be just two more pretty faces in the crowd.

Name Games

Best Name

No contest here. The best name in college football history belonged to a coach. He was Dana Xenophon Bible, and he held sway on the sidelines for some forty-five years for such schools as Texas A & M, Nebraska and Texas. His players listened carefully because "the Bible told them so."

Quoth the Raven, "Touchdown!"

Named in 1889, the first All-American football team included Princeton quarterback Edgar Allan Poe. (Yes, he was the famed writer's grandnephew. And he was not the only Poe to pass or punt for Princeton. The other Poes of Princeton included Arthur, S. Johnson, Nielson, Gresham H. and John P., Jr.)

Worst Team Names

Among the runners-up: Amherst Lord Jeffs, Delaware Fightin' Blue Hens, Oregon Ducks, Richmond Spiders, Sam Houston Bear Kats (sic), Tufts Jumbos, VMI Keydets, and the Youngstown (Ohio) State Penguins (are there Penguins in Ohio?). But the first prize goes to another Ohio powerhouse: the Akron Zips!

Scholar Athletes

The charade of big-time college athletes being passed off as genuine, serious students is a joke, if not a national disgrace. According to recently enacted NCAA standards, incoming freshmen must have a combined 700 math–verbal Scholastic Aptitude Test score (out of a possible 1,600) to be eligible. Broken down, that means the scholar athlete must correctly answer twenty-four out of eighty-five questions on the verbal portion and just thirteen of sixty on the math portion!

Once into school with these bogus scores, it takes a lot of work in classrooms to maintain academic eligibility. In order to smooth the way for its student athletes, many colleges offer, shall we say, undemanding courses. At Kansas State, for instance, football players can toil away in Music Listening Lab, in which, as you might suspect, students sit and listen to records. Then there's Georgia's Basic Instructional Media Competencies, which is the fancy way of describing how to use movie projectors and other audiovisual aids.

No More Teachers, No More Books

Big-time college coaches understand the pressures and difficulties their players face. And they are very sympathetic. Former Alabama coach Ray Perkins—recently departed for the Tampa Bay Bucs (see "Professional Football")—had this to say about the trials his players confront in trying to win football games and earn degrees. "One problem for the players is that school is going to be a distraction."

Look Out, Fridge

According to *The Guinness Book of Sports Records*, Bob Pointer, a tackle from Santa Barbara High School, once tipped the scales at 487 pounds.

The Ronald Reagan Award for Creative Sportscasting

(This award is named in honor of President Reagan's ability to simulate broadcasting a baseball game over the radio using only the wire summary of the game; this was his first documented public deception.)

When two Williams College student radio announcers showed up at Bowdoin's home field to broadcast a game between Williams and Bowdoin, they were chagrined to learn that no programs were available and they would be unable to identify the Bowdoin players. Taking their cue from the famous L.L. Bean outdoor supplier, based in nearby Freeport, Maine, they decided to use items from the catalog to call the game. Listeners soon heard reports like, ''That was a tackle by Joe Chamois Shirt.'' Substitutes were called Dick Thermal underwear and Bean Boot. When penalties were called, the infractions were converted into such abuses as ''failure to wear proper duck-hunting attire.''

Sour Notes

The marching band has a long and illustrious history in college football. If it weren't for bands playing at halftime, when else could you go to the bathroom or get something to eat? There have been many great moments in college band history, topped of course by the performance of the Stanford University band in 1982.

Band on the Run

In the eighty-fifth meeting between two archrivals, Stanford, led by John Elway, had gone ahead of California–Berkeley on a dramatic field goal. With four seconds to go, the Stanford band began "All Right Now," to celebrate the victory. Nobody noted that Cal was only fielding ten men on its return team. Golden Bear safety Kevin Moen picked up the squibbed kick, ran and then desperately lateraled to a teammate who lateraled to a third player who was apparently downed. Stanford players, fans and the band flooded the field in celebration.

But it was premature. The play had not been whistled dead. Golden Bear players kept running and lateraling, dodging players, fans, trombones and tubas. Eventually the ball found its way back to Moen, who took it all the way to the end zone, crashing through uniformed band members and upending a shocked trombonist. The officials allowed the score to stand and California's delirious home fans could not believe what they had witnessed. Nor could Stanford coach Paul Wiggin, who had this to say: "It was the biggest fiasco of all time."

In 1986 the notorious Stanford band was sent to the music room for two games for lewd and raucous behavior, including allegations that some band members had urinated on the field. Also restricted from play was the Yale band for their lewd musical numbers and marching formations in the shape of genitals.

Think You Better Slow Your Mustang Down

In another illustrious case of sour bandplay, the Mustang band of SMU was largely responsible for a 39–35 loss to archrival Texas A & M. The Mustangs were penalized 15 yards because their band was playing too loudly while Texas was calling its plays. The penalty resulted in a key first down that helped Texas to victory. If the NCAA wants to get serious about this, there are endless possibilities for band penalties. Like 5 yards whenever a band plays the theme song from *Rocky* or *2001*. Or 10 yards for any band that makes a halftime salute to their state's flower. This would also liven up halftime shows.

School for Scandal

It should come as no surprise that it was the SMU band that had been penalized. After all, this is the school that leads the nation in NCAA penalites for its recruiting atrocities. The Mustang scandals reached a crescendo in 1986 and 1987, resulting in the so-called "death penalty" from the NCAA: no SMU football in 1987, only seven games in '88; no television or bowl appearances until '89; and restrictions on recruiting and coaching staff. "My Lord," said one obviously distraught booster from Texas, where football is as dear as life itself. "They killed the program."

It was more like death by self-inflicted wounds. The NCAA investigation showed that an SMU booster had paid thirteen Mustangs $61,000 from a slush fund with the approval of key members of the SMU athletic staff. The revelations did not stop with the penalty. Newly elected Texas Governor Bill Clements admitted that, as head of SMU's board of governors, he had approved ongoing payments to players from a slush fund because they wanted to honor the commitments made to the students. But Clements denied another accusation: that SMU co-eds were paid to have sex with SMU football recruits.

When they lost their football program for 1987, SMU officials also lost their sense of humor. The school banned the campus sale of T-shirts that made fun of the school's predicament. The T-shirt in question shows the SMU Mustang lying on its back with stiff feet in the air. On the front the shirt read, "SMU Football '87" and on the back the message was "Undefeated."

Run That by Us Again, Coach

"You don't build a winning team by losing"—Ohio State coach Earle Bruce, quoted during 1986.

We Get the Point, Coach

When his Tulane football team fell to 1–3 after a tough loss in 1986, Coach Mack Brown commented, "I feel like the guy in the javelin competition who won the toss and elected to receive."

Crossed Signals: The Vince Lombardi "Winning Isn't Everything, It's the Only Thing" Trophy

High school coaches are those people we entrust to build character, teach sportsmanship and give everyone a fair shake. Apparently Mike Weaver, formerly the football coach at Langley High in McLean, Virginia, didn't get the message, so instead he gets the prize.

In a big game against Madison High, one of Mike Weaver's assistants put on a wireless radio headset and heard the distinct sound of Madison's play signals being transmitted. Weaver knew the team's terminology, so he told his assistant to stay tuned. His unsportsmanlike eavesdropping provided little help and Weaver's team lost the game 14–7. After the school's principal was told of the incident, Weaver was sacked as coach although he continues as a phys-ed teacher at the school. His reaction: "I made a bad mistake and I'm paying for it." Probably some of the school's parents are wondering what all the fuss is about. After all, McLean is home to the CIA.

More Crossed Signals: The Hot Line Heats Up

Fans of the University of Mississippi's football team, the Rebels, were eager to keep track of who the team had recruited. So in 1986 the school set up a special phone line to allow loyal followers to get regular updates on signings. But when they called the number, the football fans got another message—a female voice vividly describing another type of indoor sport. Instead of the school's number, the local paper had misprinted the number of a phone-sex fantasy service. The fans were hoping for an exciting season. Boy, did they get excitement!

Tough Guys

They say that playing scholastic football is a great character builder. The game encourages team spirit and promotes fair play. Tell that to Elizabeth Balsley. This seventeen-year-old New Jersey girl proved that she had the right stuff when she took her desire to play high school football all the way to court. The courts ruled in her favor and Elizabeth made the team. While she was far from a star, she showed grit, determination and courage in standing up for her rights and enduring the epithets and name-calling.

Some of her teammates proved less honorable. After joining the team, Balsley was roughed up after practice by three of her teammates who resented the presence of a female on the team. The three players, including the team's starting fullback, were suspended. Somehow you don't get the feeling that they really learned a lesson.

Bowled Over

What's that you say? You'd like to see more football on New Year's Day? Well, let's just bring back some of the following extinct college bowl games:

The Alamo Bowl. In one game played in 1947, Hardin–Simmons shut out Denver 20–0. The game was in honor of Jim Bowie, Davey Crockett and the Texas Rangers, who were shut out 3,500–0 by the Santa Anna Mexicans in the first annual Alamo.

The Baccardi Bowl. Played in Havana, Cuba, in 1937, the sole game ended in a 7–7 tie between Auburn and Villanova. Had there been a victor, the traditional victory champagne was to be replaced by rum and Cokes.

The Raisin Bowl. Played in Fresno, California, from 1946 to 1949, this game competed fiercely with Lodi, California's *Grape Bowl*, which ran in 1947–48.

The Salad Bowl. I kid you not. Played in Phoenix, Arizona, from 1948 to 1952.

The Lonely Bowl

They played a game of football on November 12,

1955, in Pullman, Washington. Washington State played San Jose State and the conditions were far from favorable. With high winds and a temperature of zero degrees, the game didn't attract much of a crowd. The total paid attendance was one.

CHAPTER 4

Professional Hoops

First-Round Flops

For Knicks fans, there are plenty of draft-day disasters to pick from in this category. Remember Mike Woodson, Larry Demic, Eugene Short and Dewayne Scales? They are just a few of the top Knicks picks. Go back a little farther to turn up Mel "Killer" Davis and Tom Riker. Few teams have track records as dubious or devastating as the Knicks when it comes to squandering high picks.

While the jury is still out on the Knicks' choice of Patrick Ewing, most of the other number-one picks during the past decade and a half have proven solid choices for their teams. One notable exception: Joe Barry Carroll. Taken out of Purdue by the Golden State Warriors as the overall number-one selection in the 1980 draft, Carroll was promptly tagged Joe Barry Apathy for his lackluster play.

Although named to the 1980–81 NBA All-Rookie team, it was practically by default. He had averaged 18.9 points per game and was not among the league leaders in any of the key statistical categories. During 1982–83, Carroll finally got his average up to 24.1, seventh in the league. In a contract dispute, Carroll failed to sign in '84–'85 and played in Europe instead, returning for the '85–'86 campaign when he averaged over 21 points, but Golden State still finished last in the West at 30–52.

Who exactly was selected behind Carroll in the '80 draft? Just to name a few: Kelvin Ransey, Mike O'Koren, Mike Gminski, Darrell Griffith, Andrew Toney and an ungainly forward named Kevin McHale.

Another major first-round washout was Portland's choice of LaRue Martin out of Loyola in the 1972 draft. He never made any impact on a team that finished last three straight seasons. By the time Portland became champions in 1976–77, he was no longer with the team. And the players available behind Martin? How about Paul Westphal, George McGinnis, Bob McAdoo, Julius Erving (chosen by Milwaukee but signed with the ABA) and Lucius Allen.

Defensive Struggle

On November 22, 1950, the Minneapolis Lakers, playing at home, fell to the Fort Wayne Pistons by a score of 19–18. This is the lowest scoring game in NBA history. After leading at the half by a score of 13–11, Minneapolis was able to score only 5 more points, 4 of them in the third quarter. Fort Wayne, led by guard John Oldham with 5 points, shot 4 of 13 from the field and 11 of 15 from the line. The Lakers converted only 4 of 18 shots from the field and, as in most close games, lost it on the line, where they shot 10 for 17.

Thanks, Dad

Wilt Chamberlain, certainly a contender for greatest athlete of modern times, had one notorious weakness: the man could not shoot free throws. Although he tried a variety of styles—someone even suggested starting closer to the basket and jumping backward over the foul line— and finally settled for his famous underhanded toss, the Dipper often came up short on the line. It was not for lack of practice. He was 6,057 of 11,862 from the charity stripe, by far the NBA record for free throws attempted, for an average of .511. (Among other NBA All-Time Scoring Leaders, the next worst foul shooter was Wilt's nemesis, Bill Russell, who managed to hit .561 of his free throws.) In one game in 1960, Chamberlain went 0 for 10 from the line, the most free throws attempted without making any in a single game.

It was this Achilles' heel that prompted Wilt's father to say, as Wilt was negotiating for a boxing match with Muhammad Ali in 1971: "You'd be better off if you gave back those gloves right now and went down to the gym and worked on foul shots."

Liquid-Chocolate Centers

March 2, 1962. It was a night that Darrall Imhoff and Dave Budd will probably never forget. Or live down. Playing for the Knicks against Philadelphia at Hershey, Pennsylvania, they were the opposing centers who melted in Wilt's hands on the night that Chamberlain scored 100 points in the 169–147 Philly victory. Imhoff played twenty minutes before fouling out with 7 points. Bud avoided foul trouble by switching to a wear-him-down defense in which he apparently thought that Chamberlain's arms would eventually tire from taking all those shots. All sports records are made to be broken, but Chamberlain's amazing performance that night is one that may stand the test of time.

Basketball's Worst Trades

There are plenty of stinkers in the trading annals of the NBA; and remember, one man's worst trade is almost always another's key to a championship. That was certainly the case when the Detroit Pistons traded **Dave DeBusschere** to New York during the 1968–69 season. Detroit's top pick in 1962, the burly forward had been a rebounding and defensive mainstay for the Pistons. But in a New York uniform, he was the missing link on the team that broke Boston's dominance of the Atlantic Division in 1969–70. Playing in the front court with Willis Reed and Bill Bradley, DeBusschere anchored two championship Knick teams and put up Hall of Fame statistics.

Remember who Detroit got in return for DeBusschere? **Walt Bellamy** and **Howard (Butch) Komives.** At the time, it looked as if Detroit had gotten the best of the deal. Bellamy was among the league's leading scorers and rebounders while Komives was a good assist man. But while DeBusschere was helping to hang flags in the Garden, Komives played for Detroit for several solid but unspectacular years and Bellamy was traded away to Atlanta during the 1969–70 season.

The trading of **Julius Erving** is an even sadder case, and if there is a hell for owners, former New York Net owner Roy Boe must be sweating it out. The Doctor had been one of the superstars of the American Basketball Association. When the NBA absorbed four ABA teams in 1976, Erving was expected to become a superstar of the first rank in the NBA. In fact, having Dr. J play in NBA buildings may have been one of the reasons the established league agreed to the merger at all. But after leading the Nets to consecutive ABA titles, Erving was sold to the Philadelphia 76ers for $4 million, supposedly the Nets' entry fee into the NBA. It was a loss from which the Nets never truly recovered. Erving was not only the team's offensive leader, he was its soul. With his departure, the Nets slipped into the obscurity of the New Jersey swamps. (It can be said that Erving was also involved in another of the worst swaps in basketball history when he was traded to the Nets by the Virginia Squires for **George Carter,** draft rights to Kermit Washington and cash.)

More recently, the multiplayer swap between Washington and Philadelphia prior to the 1986–87 season has the look of a train wreck for Philly. Sixers owner Harold Katz gave up **Moses Malone** for **Jeff Ruland.** Discounting the exchange of draft picks and other players involved (Philly got **Cliff Robinson** while Washington got **Terry Catledge** as part of the deal), the Malone-for-Ruland deal smelled of rotten fish in Philly, especially with an aging Dr. J on the verge of retirement. Ruland, injury-plagued for most of his career, spent much of the 1986–87 season in street clothes and just after the season ended was forced to retire. Shrugging off his injuries, Moses led Washington into the playoffs while boosting Washington's sagging attendance and lifting the team's often somnolent style of play.

Dubious Achievements
(Stats They'll Never Write Home About)

Records-We'd-Rather-Not-Have Department

In February 1987 the Sacramento Kings set several new records for offensive futility in a 128–92 loss to the L.A. Lakers. The Lakers spurted to a 29–0 start (a league record) and the first quarter ended with the Kings down by 40–4 (a league record first-quarter low score that also tied the NBA low for a single quarter). The Kings went 0 for 18 from the field as their only first-quarter points came from the free-throw line. Kings coach Phil Johnson said afterward, "It's a good thing we're a good free throw–shooting team." Kings player Derek Smith commented, "It didn't take an Einstein to realize that when they were up by 16 points and were running plays for Kurt Rambis to hit jump shots, we were in trouble."

That Chump-ionship Season:
★ Most Losses

Remember the 1972–73 NBA season? The Knicks do. That was when they won their second NBA championship. "Tiny" Archibald does, too. He became the first man to lead the league in both scoring and assists. For other reasons, the **Philadelphia 76ers** of 1972–73 will never forget that campaign, even though they would dearly love to do just that. The Philly team—featuring Fred Carter, Kevin Loughery, Manny Leaks, Leroy Ellis and an aging Hal Greer in his last season—finished up this season of glory with a 9–73 record, a "winning percentage" of .110. They ended up fifty-nine games behind Boston in the Atlantic Division, scoring an average of 104.1 points per game while allowing 116.2 p.p.g.

★ Fewest Wins

While the futility of the '72 Philly squad surely ranks as the worst team performance in NBA history, not far behind are the **Providence Steamrollers** of 1947–48. "Steamrolled" would have been a more appropriate name as the team was flattened by just about everyone in the league, ending up with a 6–42 record, a "winning percentage" of .125. They finished up twenty-one games behind the Philadelphia Warriors and the roster was highlighted by such memorable NBA greats as Ernie Calverley, George Nostrand, Kenneth Sailors and Earl Shannon. Providence doubled its win total in the 1948–49 season as the league went to a sixty-game schedule. However, that was the last of the Steamrollers. The team folded after the season as the NBA expanded in 1949–50 to seventeen teams playing a sixty-four-game schedule. The enlarged league included the Anderson Packers, Chicago Stags, Fort Wayne Pistons, Indianapolis Olympians, Rochester Royals, St. Louis Bombers, Sheboygan Redskins, Syracuse Nationals, Tri-Cities Blackhawks and Waterloo Hawks.

Personal Fouls

Career: **Kareem Abdul-Jabbar,** already the league leader in six statistical categories, added the fouling crown to his collection during a game in March 1987. His fourth-quarter personal against Danny Schayes was number 4,194. Asked about his achievement, The Big Guy commented, "Yeah, but half of them were bad calls." Kareem finished the 1986–87 season with 4,245 fouls, moving him well past the previous whistle-blowing king, Elvin Hayes. Best known as the Big E, Hayes could just as well be called the Big F. Between 1968 in San Diego and 1984 in Houston, Elvin Hayes accounted for 4,193 whistles being blown. He is followed by Hal Greer, who racked up 3,855 between 1958 and 1973.

Season: **Darryl Dawkins,** aka Chocolate Thunder from the Planet Lovetron, picked up 386 fouls during the 1983–84 season for the New Jersey Nets. Double D is also second on the list with 379 fouls committed during the previous season, also while playing for New Jersey.

Single game: **Don Otten,** playing for the Tri-Cities Blackhawks, was whistled eight times in a 1949 game against the Sheboygan Redskins. Of course, this dubious achievement will never be equaled, as it occurred prior to the six-fouls disqualification rule.

Playoffs: **Arnie Risen** of Boston (1957) and **Tom Sanders** of Boston (1965) both committed thirty-seven fouls during a seven-game series.

Fouling Out (Disqualifications began in the 1950–51 season.)

Career: **Vern Mikkelsen,** who led the league in fouls

while playing for Minneapolis in consecutive seasons from 1954 to 1958, was whistled out of 127 games.

Season: **Don Meineke,** playing with Fort Wayne in 1952–53, fouled out of twenty-six games. Among active players, **Steve Johnson** of Kansas City got the boot twenty-five times in 1981–82 and **Dawkins** took twenty-three early showers in 1982–83 for New Jersey.

Playoffs: **Arnie Risen** of Boston (1957, seven games) and **Charlie Scott,** also of Boston (1976, six games), both fouled out five times.

Turnovers (Statistics compiled since 1977–78 season.)

Career: **Moses Malone** coughed it up 2,711 times between 1977 and the 1986–87 season

Season: **Artis Gilmore** gave up the ball 366 times while playing for Chicago in the 1977–78 season.

Single game: **John Drew**—14 (Atlanta at New Jersey, March 1978).

Playoffs: **Charles Barkley** of Philadelphia turned the ball over 37 times during a seven-game series in 1986.

Longest Losing Streak

The aforementioned **Philadelphia 76ers** set the NBA standard for a schneid when they dropped twenty straight between January and February 1973. That same season, Philly dropped fifteen straight to start the season. Hot on their heels with nineteen-loss skeins are the 1981–82 **Cleveland Cavaliers,** also known as the "Cadavers," and the 1981–82 **Clippers,** then located in San Diego. The longest losing streak over combined seasons is **Cleveland**'s string of twenty-four losses, which included the last nineteen games in 1982 and the first five games in 1983.

Oh-fer Goodness Sake

Seven times players in the NBA have gone 0 for 15 from the field in a single game. However, Philadelphia's **Howie Dallmar** is the only man to have done it twice—once in 1947 and again in 1948. Most recently, this incredible sure-shooting feat was performed by **Ray Williams** playing for New Jersey in 1981 against Indiana.

Road Warriors

The **Baltimore Bullets** of 1953–54 went 0–20 on the road. Combined with the twelve road games lost in the previous season, the team also earns honors for most consecutive road losses with thirty-two.

Playoff Drought

Some good things, like fine wines, take a long time to come of age. Ask the **Indiana Pacers**. After eleven years of futile waiting, they finally did it—they actually won an NBA playoff game. Prior to the 1987 playoffs, the Pacers had only made one NBA playoff appearance. That came during the 1980–81 Eastern Conference first-round series when they were swept by the Philadelphia 76ers in two games. In the '87 playoffs, after two opening losses against Dominique Wilkins and the Atlanta Hawks, the Pacers came back to win game three by a score of 96–87. It was a small moral victory as the Hawks then eliminated the Pacers by three games to one.

Football's Got the Super Bowl, but Basketball Has Manute Bol

Is there a stranger sight in all of sports than Manute Bol? The 7'6" center for the Washington Bullets came to the United States from Africa to play basketball at the University of Bridgeport. In his single year at Bridgeport, Bol got plenty of attention, but his basketball talents were primarily limited to blocking shots. After a summer season with the Rhode Island Gulls of the USBL (where one of his teammates was 5'7" Spud Webb), Bol was signed by the Washington Bullets. Following Bol's rookie season, Washington knew it had to bulk up the spindly center before the wear and tear of the NBA pivot cracked the Bol.

In the summer of 1986, Bol measured in at 7'6" weighing 187 pounds (with a body fat ratio of 8.8 percent). At that time he was capable of doing two push-ups. By the fall of 1986, after a regimen of weight training and nutritional counseling, Bol had gained one-half inch, was up to 230 pounds and his body fat had increased to 18.2 percent. He was capable of ten push-ups.

Still, Bol's basketball basics needed some additional polishing. In the 1986–87 season, Bol went 692 minutes (five months into the season) before recording his first assist of the year when he passed to Moses Malone and Malone scored. Following this belated achievement, Bol remarked, "What do you expect? I'm not Magic Johnson."

Name Games

We Are the World

Lloyd B. Free seemed like a nice enough name for the free-shooting guard with the Philadelphia 76ers. Never known for being too shy to shoot, Free went by the nickname "All World." Liking the ring of that, Free legally changed his name to World B. Free. After barrel-bottom-scraping stints with the San Diego Clippers, the Golden State Warriors and Cleveland Cavaliers, he was freed by the Cavaliers during the '86–'87 season. A free agent, World went back to Philadelphia for twenty games and was cut. That's the way of the World.

Worst Nickname

While World was certainly an unusual name, it did have a certain style to it, a bit of panache. The same cannot be said for Marvin Webster's nickname. While playing at Morgan State, Webster was one of college's leading shot blockers and was christened with the ungainly title of "The Human Eraser," a name Webster certainly never considered adopting as his legal name.

The center for the Western Division champion Seattle Supersonics in 1977–78, Webster came to the Knicks as a free agent in the next season and probably grew to hate the name as it became apparent that his talents had been mysteriously erased upon his arrival in New York.

Worst Team Names

Just as players have been stuck with ungainly names, so have whole teams. Capricious owners, unusual moves from one city to another and dumb franchise-naming fan contests have all contributed to the strange collection of names in NBA history. It is kind of hard to imagine, for instance, any name being right for a team from Sheboygan. (The Sheboygan Redskins played in 1949–50 and lasted one season.) The Tri-Cities Blackhawks, another 1950s vintage team, also sounds pretty bogus, more like an industrial softball team than an NBA franchise.

Then there are the current teams. For instance, what does Los Angeles have to do with lakes? Nothing. But the Lakers was a perfect name for a team from Minneapolis, Minnesota, the land of 10,000 lakes. When the franchise moved west in 1960, the name stuck with them.

Another example of a team name suffering from a move came when the NBA's New Orleans franchise headed west for Salt Lake City. The Jazz was a perfectly good name for a team in New Orleans. But the Utah Jazz? Come on. Is there a town anywhere else in America with less syncopation than Salt Lake City, home of the Mormon Tabernacle Choir? As winner of the worst team name in the NBA, the Utah Jazz is the perfect definition of an oxymoron—a word that contradicts itself, like "military intelligence" or "postal service." Now, if the New Orleans football franchise had moved to Utah—and there are plenty of Louisiana football fans who wish they would do just that—the Salt Lake Saints would make perfect sense. And they would be right at home in the desert.

Fun Couple

Nancy Lieberman and Michael Ray Richardson, backcourt teammates for the Long Island Knights of the USBL. The All-American from Queens, New York, and Old Dominion, Lieberman was nicknamed "Lady Magic" after she braved the playgrounds of Harlem. She later became Martina Navratilova's housemate, physical training coach and "spiritual counselor." Lieberman also became the first woman to play in a men's professional league. (The first woman ever drafted by the NBA team was Anne Meyers, cut in camp by the Indiana Pacers.)

In an intriguing backcourt combination, Lieberman was joined on the team by Richardson, the three-time loser who was banned from NBA action for his repeated cocaine use. Their relationship was brief as the troubled Richardson failed to see eye-to-eye with team management and moved on to join the Jersey Jammers.

Motta Mouth

Would a professional basketball team tank a game to set up a more favorable playoff schedule? Apparently they would, according to Dallas Maverick coach Dick Motta. At the close of the 1986–87 season Motta accused his Texas rivals, the Houston Rockets, of "messing around" on the court to avoid the same playoff bracket as the Los Angeles Lakers. Motta's comments followed a Rockets–Phoenix Suns game in which the trailing Rockets closed to within 2 poinds of the Suns in the fourth quarter but kept their best players on the bench. "Houston looks like they're messing around," charged Motta. "They look like they're manipulating. . . . It was about the most blatant I've ever seen. It wasn't even cute. It's a good thing he [Bill Fitch] has a two-year extension. Thirty-seven victories isn't enough for most people to hold a job.''

In rebuttal, Houston coach Bill Fitch said, "He must have been thinking about when he was a ninth-grade coach in Idaho, because he brought some ninth-grade thinking with those statements.'' The charges did not amuse the NBA, which suspended Motta for a game and fined the Mavericks $5,000 after its investigation into the affair concluded Fitch and the Rockets had done nothing wrong.

An Earful

Boston Celtic announcer Johnny Most is as much a part of the tradition in Boston Garden as the parquet floor, the banners above and the retired jerseys. His "Havlicek stole the ball" cry is a part of sports broadcasting legend. But during the 1987 season, he went to Celtic team doctor Thomas Silva complaining of hearing difficulties. Silva checked out Most's ear and found an old earplug. "That must have been there from when I worked with SportsChannel," said Most. That occasion had come nearly a year before.

Accidents Will Happen

If the 1986–87 Los Angeles Clippers were a Broadway show, they would have closed during previews. This was a *bad* team. The team should have known it was going to be a rocky year when the first of two crippling accidents struck—before the season and off the court. Guard Norm

Nixon was playing softball in Central Park when he stepped in a hole and ruptured a tendon in his left knee, costing him the season.

Two weeks into the season, the fickle finger of fate struck again. Forward Marques Johnson came down with a rebound and turned his head into the substantial stomach of center Benoit Benjamin. He ruptured a cervical disk, was lost for the season and his future career was left in question.

For his part, Benjamin thought that a few extra pounds might help out in taking the pounding of the NBA pivot. He showed up at Clipper training camp nearly thirty pounds overweight. His thighs were so fat, they had to be lubed with Vaseline to prevent chapping. ''Most of my weight is liquid,'' said Benjamin. A former teammate, Cedric Maxwell, had a different perspective on the young center's girth: ''If Benoit hadn't eaten in two days and he was thrown into a cage with a grizzly, you can rest assured *somebody* would get a fur coat.''

Foul Lines

Teamwork

''My biggest thrill came the night Elgin Baylor and I combined for 73 points in Madison Square Garden. Elgin had 71 of them.''—Former Laker Hot Rod Hundley.

Maybe That's Why You're in Jersey, Leon

Upon meeting television sportscaster Steve Albert, New Jersey Nets guard Leon Wood queried, ''Are you any relation to your brother Marv?''

Maybe That's Why You're in Jersey, Chris

In his first game against the Celtics in 1983, Net rookie Chris Engler was playing against former U. of Minnesota roommate and friend Kevin McHale. As they ran upcourt, McHale told his old friend, "When you get the ball, just move in close and shoot a jumper. I won't block it. I want to make you look good." When he got the ball, Engler followed McHale's suggestion. "Next thing I know, Kevin was slapping the ball off my forehead. He smiled and said, 'I lied.' "

White Man's Burden

After seeing his playing time cut by coach Bob Hill, Knicks forward Pat Cummings complained that he would begrudgingly accept the coach's decision, but it wasn't much fun. Hill, the 1987 midseason replacement for Hubie Brown, replied, "I have a lot of trouble with guys who can't run and jump." So do Knicks fans.

Low Post-er

Speaking of New York Knicks fans, did you hear about the 1987 St. Patrick's Day in Madison Square Garden? As a promotion, the Knicks gave out life-sized posters of seven-footer Patrick Ewing. Unfortunately, it was an off night for Ewing as he played a mediocre game in another New York loss (to Denver). Disgusted New York fans decided to return the posters and did so during the game, sending their freebies cascading onto the court. The next day *Daily News* columnist Mike Lupica noted, "Patrick Ewing is lucky it wasn't Bat Day."

Texas Chain Saw Massacre, Part III

After watching a halftime show featuring a man juggling chain saws, Dallas Maverick player personnel director Rick Sund commented, "You have a turnover there, and you've got trouble."

Court Date

Speaking of weird halftime shows, there is the Denver radio station's annual Nugget Nuptials contest. Q103-FM listeners are invited to send postcard entries for a lottery drawing. First prize: a halftime wedding ceremony on Valentine's Day in front of 17,000 Nuggets fans. "It's a wild time," said an official of the station. "When the judge asks, 'Does anyone know of a reason why these two shouldn't be married?' some guys always start yelling, 'Yes! Yes! Don't do it.' " In addition to the ceremony, the winners receive wedding bands—presumably not cast from old basketball rims—a night in a local hotel's honeymoon suite and a week in Acapulco along with good seats to the game and 100 extra tickets for guests.

CHAPTER 5

School and College Hoops

Don't Bet On It

"Gamblers couldn't get at my boys with a ten-foot pole." Kentucky's legendary coach Adolph Rupp said it in the midst of the point-shaving scandals of the late forties that saw players from Manhattan College and the City College of New York involved in fixing points in games played from 1947–51. Apparently the gamblers did not bother with a long pole but used short, thick rolls of cash. Three Kentucky players from the 1949 NCAA championship team, Beard, Barnstable, and Groza, admitted losing the National Invitational Tournament final to Loyola on purpose.

Scholar Athletes, Part I

In the Oklahoma University 1986 basketball media guide under the subject of "Favorite Class," Sooner forward Darryl (Choo) Kennedy listed "Theory of Basketball."

Scholar Athletes, Part II

The end of the Lloyd Daniels story is yet to be written. One hopes it will be a "happy" ending, with the court prodigy becoming one of the country's highest-paid functional illiterates for his ability to put a ball through a hoop. The dubious-distinction part of his plight, however, does not belong to this schoolboy who never finished high school. Instead it goes to the so-called "educators" who saw Daniels as a prize to be won at any cost; among them a variety of New York City high school coaches who wrangled over which school Daniels could play for without much regard for his academic situation. One of his "academic advisors" liked to bet the ponies and used to take Daniels to local New York tracks.

Coach Jerry "Tark the Shark" Tarkanian of UNLV had one of his assistants become Daniels's legal guardian and financial advisor while the boy was sent to a junior college where he could play basketball until he was ready to be accepted as a transfer to UNLV. Among his courses at Mount San Antonio JC: basketball, Fundamentals of Sports–Basketball, a recreation class, strength and conditioning, and an ethnic-studies course. Unable to read, Daniels actually made the dean's list at the school based on these courses. Said one of his instructors: "Lloyd did all right. There was no heavy reading. Just say they were activity courses."

Caught in a police bust of a "crack house" in 1987, Daniels was dropped like a hot potato from the UNLV basketball program and was recently sentenced to probation. But that hasn't stopped plenty of other NCAA coaches from calling Las Vegas to express their interest in recruiting the schoolboy basketball whiz.

Heavy Course Load

The dubious academic requirements of major universities is well documented. At the above-mentioned UNLV—best known for its School of Hotel Management, which provides future casino employees with courses in gambling—the basketball team is sometimes able to combine business with pleasure. Recently seven UNLV Rebels took a social-work course called "Contemporary Issues in Social Welfare" for as many as six credits. The course required each player to read, submit term papers and spend several hours on field trips. Oh, yes. They were taking this specially arranged course during a sixteen-day playing tour of New Zealand, Australia and Tahiti.

You Don't Have to be Schvartze to Love Basketball

After scoring 24 points against Georgia Tech in a 1986 game, Penn's Bruce Lefkowitz said, "I guess they're not used to seeing slow, white Jewish guys in the ACC."

You Don't Have to Be Schvartze, II

When the boys of the Miami Hebrew Academy suited up for a game, they wore their yarmulkes, just like all Orthodox Jewish boys. But the referees, clinging to the rule book as if it were the Talmud, said the head coverings were against the regulation forbidding headgear. Rather than forsake the yarmulkes, required by their faith, the boys refused to play and the game was postponed. With Solomon-like wisdom, the team came up with the idea of attaching their yarmulkes to their headbands and were allowed to return to the court. Jim McMahon would have loved that one!

NC Double A, Double Standard

According to the rules of the NCAA, college players are prohibited from appearing in any advertisement or commercial venture, whether it is for profit or charity. Steve Alford, the guard from Indiana, learned that lesson the hard way when he appeared in a sorority poster that was being used to raise funds for charity. The NCAA forced Alford to sit out a couple of games. But every week of the college football or basketball season, television uses pictures of NCAA athletes to promote upcoming telecasts. What's the difference? Simple. The television money goes into the NCAA coffers and the NCAA is not going to bite the hand that feeds it by telling its television partners not to use the athletes to promote the games. That is hypocrisy in action.

Name Games

What the Hell Is a Hoya, Anyway?

According to the Georgetown basketball yearbook, ''In the days when all Georgetown students were required to study Greek and Latin, the University's teams were nicknamed The Stonewalls. A student, using Latin and Greek terms, started the cheer 'Hoya Saxa' which translates 'What Rocks!' The name proved popular and the name Hoyas was eventually adopted for all Georgetown teams.''

Worst College Team Nickname

No question. The Horned Frogs of Texas Christian University. Image being able to tell your grandchildren that you were once a Horned Frog!

Best Name

In the 1987 NCAA Tournament, the NBA found a prospect, and an unforgettably named one at that: Wyoming Cowboys forward Fennis Dembo.

Equal Fights for Women, or Bad Girls Get Discipline

On January 17, 1987, the women of the University of Missouri and Oklahoma made college basketball history by engaging in the first bench-clearing brawl in a women's game. Missouri AD Jack Lengyel later said that two members of the team would be disciplined for their retaliatory action in the game.

Girls in Chains, or More Girls Get Discipline

''We want to do something different to get the attention of the kids in school and bring the people out to games,'' said coach Tom May of the Crown Point (Indiana) High School girls' team. ''It's mainly a promotional device, but we also use it as a teaching tool.'' The so-called promotional device is a twenty-pound ball and chain that May requires the girl with the poorest stats to carry around for a day following each game, win or lose.

May's methods, like the Marquis de Sade's, get results. The chain gang has compiled a 146–22 record under the coach and won state championships in 1984 and 1985. According to one report, the girls seem to crave the dubious honor. "I think it really helps," said one player, "and it makes you want to eliminate mistakes." It is not known if May is considering making *The Story of O* required reading for next year's team.

Wilted Roses

Thank goodness May's chain gang technique is not put to use at the Sacred Heart school in Carbondale, Pennsylvania. According to *Sports Illustrated*, the Lady Roses basketball team had gone five and one-half seasons without a win, a losing streak of 120 straight games. The team has not won since 1981. Their moral victory came in the final game of 1987 when they lost 75–32 to undefeated Riverside. In the final quarter of the game, the Lady Roses scored 13 points, one more than Riverside in that period. It marked the first time that season that Sacred Heart had outscored an opponent in any period.

Seesaw Battle

It took a full regulation game and then three overtimes and still there was no winner. It was March 1925, a game pitting two girls' high school teams in North Dakota. After the overtimes, the score remained knotted at 0–0. The ref decided to take the game into his own hands. He flipped a coin. Kensal High called heads and won the toss and the game.

Combat Reporters

Sports reporting often uses combat language, but rarely do reporters need helmets and flak jackets. Unless they work for the *Lexington Herald-Leader*. After running a series of articles about improper payments to players in the Kentucky basketball program, the paper received its expected 800 subscriber cancellations. What they didn't expect was the rash of bomb threats that forced the evacuation of the newspaper's offices.

Coke Isn't It

Michael Wilson must have thought he was pretty lucky when he won a contest in which the prize was a trip to the NCAA Final Four showdown in 1987. Unfortunately, the contest was sponsored by Pepsi, and Wilson worked for Coke. When his Coke bosses advised him not to accept the prize, hoop fan Wilson told them exactly where they could stick it. He lost his job. That was the bad news. The good news was that Wilson then joined the Pepsi Generation when Coke's rival heard of his plight and offered him a job to go along with his trip.

Coke Isn't It, Part II

America's favorite liquid refreshmen made news in other ways during the 1987 NCAA Championship. In the year that postgame drug testing was done for the first time, players were chosen to represent their teams at the urinals. Often dehydrated after a couple of hours of basketball, many players were not able to give their all to the NCAA loving cups. More concerned with drug testing than with the health of the players, NCAA officials insisted upon forcing the players to drink large quantities of liquids, including Coke. In at least one instance, the forcible-drinking policy made players sick to their stomachs when two St. John's players became nauseated after being given six glasses of Coke.

Smoke Gets in Your Eyes

The NCAA drug testing policy not only made some players sick, it caused others to change their sleeping arrangements. The University of Florida team, coached by Norm Sloan, was encamped at a Syracuse hotel for its first-round games at Syracuse's Carrier Dome. Two Florida players, Vernon Maxwell and Andrew Moten, informed their coach that marijuana was being smoked in the room next to theirs. Afraid of "secondary marijuana smoking" getting into his players' systems and showing up during testing, Sloan had the entire team moved to another hotel.

The Gators' partying neighbors were part of a large ski tour contingent staying at the hotel and apparently they did not have to worry about drug testing after a few hours on the slopes. Said Sloan: "When I got on the elevator this morning, there was a guy standing there in a bathing suit and ski boots. He had a smile on his face. He was prepared to go to the beach or the mountains. He had enough alcohol in him not to freeze."

Some People Never Learn

In 1987, almost a year after the death of former Maryland star player Len Bias, Lefty Dreisell, Bias's college coach, told a conference that cocaine could enhance athletic performance. Dreisell later apologized and said his remarks were misconstrued. With remarks like that, Dreisell should draw a couple of technicals and be benched, permanently.

Nature's Call

When Austin Peay (pronounced "pea") advanced in the 1987 NCAA tourney, it made for some interesting crowd chants. Fans of the small school loudly and clearly exhorted the team to "Let's Go Peay." It is not known whether this exuberance caused massive tie-ups in the bathrooms.

Pass the Water

Austin's Peay-call brings to mind one of the great dubious moments in basketball broadcasting history. North Carolina State was in the Garden for the NIT Tournament back in 1951. Veteran broadcaster Marty Glickman would be calling the game and, pro that he is, Glickman wanted to check the pronunciation of the players' names prior to the tip-off. He checked with the N.C. State coach about one player in particular, Bernie Yurin, and the coach told Glickman it sounds the way it's spelled.

For Glickman it was a night of embarrassed amusement as he tried to put a good face on things, but his calls of "Yurin dribbles" and "Yurin's hot tonight" had Glickman and his fellow announcer laughing so hard that, well, to put it one way, they almost wet their pants.

"And They Sure Can Dance...."

Glickman's embarrassment was innocent compared to

the remarks made by CBS announcer Tom Brookshier, who could have given tact lessons to Al Campanis (see "Baseball"). Talking about the 1983 Louisville team, Brookshier commented; "Denny Crum has a great team at Louisville. They have a collective IQ of about 40. But they can play basketball." Louisville, a national audience, the NCAA and CBS were not amused and Brookshier's on-the-air season was finished.

Knight Work

The unhappy subject of the best-selling book *Season on the Brink*, Indiana coach Bobby Knight called the book's author, John Feinstein, a "pimp" and a "whore." Feinstein's response: "I wish he'd make up his mind so I'd know how to dress."

A Knightmare

Following Indiana's victory in the 1987 NCAA Championship, Michael Jordan, a teammate of Hoosier Steve Alford on the Olympic team coached by Knight, said: "I owe him [Alford] $100 right now because I told him I never thought he'd stay four years with Bobby Knight." (See Bobby Knight in "Foul Plays Hall of Fame.")

CHAPTER 6

Blood Sports: Hockey, Boxing, Professional Wrestling

Hockey

The Rodney Dangerfield line about "going to a fight only to have a hockey game break out" is no longer funny. The National Hockey League goes through a seemingly endless eighty-game season, filled with bullying, slashing and spearing, in order to eliminate a handful of teams; the other teams qualifying for the equally endless Stanley Cup playoffs. NHL highlight films look more and more like street brawls. There's nothing new about this. A long time ago, sportswriter Jimmy Cannon defined a hockey puck as "a hard rubber disk that hockey players strike when they can't hit one another."

But in recent years, fed by television replays of fights, fans that seem to glory in bloodletting and a league office that gives fighting its blessing with meaningless fines, the hockey match has deteriorated. These days, as Frank Deford of *Sports Illustrated* put it, "Hockey is the only place where a guy can go and watch two white guys fight."

Loving Cup

If the NHL has become a maelstrom of violent boys looking for a fight, Philadelphia is the center of the storm. The Broad Street Bullies have elevated their street-fighting tactics to a longtime tradition. But the Flyers set a new low for even the NHL during the 1987 Stanley Cup playoffs: a massive fight on the ice **before the game even began!**

The incident came during the semifinals between Philadelphia and the Montreal Canadiens, the 1985–86 Stanley Cup winners. It started as a Flyer response to an irritating Montreal pregame ritual. The Flyers had grown increasingly annoyed as Canadien right winger Claude Lemieux completed his warmups by shooting a puck into the empty Philadelphia net—a technical violation of a rule calling for a separation of teams during warmups. With the ice practically empty, this superstitious act seemed inconsequential. But not to the Flyers.

So in game six, the Flyers let the gorillas out of their cages. When Lemieux and teammate Shayne Corson skated toward the empty Flyer net, they were shadowed by the Flyers' Ed Hospodar, a marginal player, and Chico Resch, the backup goal tender. As Corson took a shot, Resch slid his stick along the ice and Hospodar punched Lemieux repeatedly. Soon the rest of the two teams returned to the ice to take up the battle as astonished Forum workers trying to prepare the rink watched. In their dressing room, the referees were unaware of the fight, and it went on for about ten minutes. At least four fights followed the initial confrontation. All the while television cameras kept rolling. One league official and the backup referee watched without intervening and the game began without penalties!

The day after the Flyers beat the Canadiens, the NHL announced the punishment: a total of $24,500 in fines split six ways—"Beer money" in the words of writer George Vecsey—and the suspension of only Hospodar from the Cup finals.

Dubious Achievements

Coldest Streak

With a 5–4 win over the Colorado Rockies on December 23, 1980, a painful period in **Winnipeg Jets** history came to a merciful close. The team had gone thirty games without a victory, a stretch of futility that saw their record go 0–23 with seven ties. During that schneid, the Jets went through three coaches, Tom McVie, Bill Sutherland and Mike Smith, who, to the surprise of the sports world, was not rehired after the season.

The Baddest Boys: Most Penalty Minutes

Single game: Playing for the Los Angeles Kings, **Randy Holt** was hit for 67 minutes in a game against Philadelphia on March 1, 1979.

Single season: Best known as **"The Hammer," Dave Schultz,** who played primarily with the Flyers, piled up an all-time high of 472 penalty minutes during the 1975 season. That surpassed his own record of 348 set in 1974. (After his retirement, Schultz wrote a book condemning hockey violence.)

Lifetime: He started in 1974 and is still going strong. Through the 1986–87 season, **Dave "Tiger" Williams** acquired 3,879 minutes of time in the box while playing with Toronto, Vancouver and Los Angeles. Of Williams, the subject of the book *Tiger—A Hockey Story,* veteran hockey reporter Tim Moriarty said, "He's a wise guy. Crude and intolerant. He loves to insult and degrade female reporters. He's not fond of male reporters either."

Name Games

Hockey's Least Likely Name

Playing for Buffalo from 1978 to 1985 and then for Los Angeles was a gentleman named Larry Playfair. This 6'4", 220-pound defenseman has compiled a long and impressive list of on-the-ice conquests. Maybe he should adopt a motto: "Playfair. Fight Dirty."

Hockey's Worst Nickname

Georges Vezina was the legendary goalie for Montreal for whom the Vezina Trophy, presented each year to the NHL's leading goalie, is named. Thank goodness they didn't decide to use Vezina's nickname for the award. Vezina went through his long career with the cumbersome and unsightly nickname "The Chicoutimi Cucumber." Really rolls off the tongue, doesn't it?

A Nice Bunch of Fans

During the 1987 Stanley Cup playoffs between the Philadelphia Flyers and the New York Rangers, Philly fans booed the arrival of a stretcher to remove an injured Ranger player.

Cherry Pits

Hockey fans can be an unforgiving bunch. Ask Don Cherry. When fired as coach of the sad-sack Colorado Rockies, Cherry commented: "I'm happy I wasn't around for the Crucifixion, because I would have gotten blamed for that."

Pennies From Heaven

According to *The Complete Handbook of Pro Hockey*, Detroit Red Wing coach Jacques Demers is "firm, friendly and honest" and "a veritable genius." Demers demonstrated his genius and honesty in splendid fashion during a 1986 playoff game while coaching the St. Louis Blues. There was a break in the action and the ice was being prepared for the next period. Demers felt that his players could use a little extra time to get their wind. His solution: he threw five pennies on the ice which arena workers then had to remove. In the truest NHL tradition of anything goes, Demers was not penalized for his coin toss.

You Can't Take Them Anywhere

After a loss to the North Stars early in the '87 campaign, several members of the Toronto Maple Leafs apparently tried to drown their sorrows. Unfortunately, they were also drowning out everything else. As a result, their hotel in Bloomington, Minnesota, asked the five players to leave. The five ended up spending the night at a diner. If that's what the Leafs do when they lose, watch out if they ever win.

Boxing

A. J. Liebling called it "The Sweet Science." But today's fight game is neither sweet nor very scientific. As former heavyweight fighter Ken Norton put it, "Boxing is a great sport and a dirty business." Too Tall Jones, who left the Dallas cowboys for an aborted stint as a boxer, held an equally disenchanted view: "I have never been around so many crummy people in all my days."

Short and Sweet

On September 23, 1946, Al Couture knocked out Ralph Walton in ten and one-half seconds—including the ten-second count. Couture hit his opponent while Walton was in his corner adjusting his mouthpiece.

The quickest fight recorded was a 1947 Golden Gloves bout in Minneapolis that lasted only four seconds when Mike Colins one-punched Pat Brownson to the canvas and the match was halted without a count.

Punched-Out Clocks

What's a few seconds here or there? Apparently not much in the world of boxing timekeepers. While the rules state that rounds should last three minutes, it's apparently anybody's count that rings the bell. In one notorious instance, the Gerrie Coetzee–Michael Dokes title fight in 1984, the rounds were about two seconds longer than the regulations call for. If time had been kept accurately, Dokes should have been in his corner when he was knocked out at 2:58 of the tenth round. In extremes, timekeepers have been off by as much as a minute, according to *The Guinness Sports Record Book 1987–88*. One boxing official commented: "With all the excitement, it's sometimes hard to keep exact time."

Roped In

There may have been better heavyweights than Muhammad Ali, but there is no doubt that he was the world's most recognizable heavyweight champion and certainly the greatest showman in modern boxing. His shadow still lingers over the heavyweight division. Unfortunately for Ali, his luck outside the ring hasn't equaled his greatness on the canvas. After earning some $55 million in the ring. Ali has let millions disappear into the hands of hangers-on who have brought shady business deals into the Champ's camp. Apparently afflicted with Parkinson's syndrome, a brain disorder that slurs his speech and slows his movements, the bighearted Ali has fallen prey to a number of misguided schemers. One of the ventures capitalizing on his name was Champion Brand shoe polish, a product that resulted in a trademark infringement suit and was the idea of Arthur Morrison, an Ali associate who turned out to be a fugitive from an attempted burglary warrant. Another scheme, Ali Motors, has attempted to create cars—the 3WC, for Three

World Championships, and a Brazilian car, the Stinger—neither of which has gotten off the ground. Finally there was Champion Sports Management, a boxing camp that collapsed when the man running it, Richard Hirschfeld, violated securities laws.

Yet to hit the market: Champ Gourmet Chocolate Cookies.

Where the Money Wasn't

Ali's recent deals bring to mind that his name was involved in one of boxing's most dubious adventures—the strange case of Harold Smith. Appearing out of nowhere in 1979, Smith secured the use of Ali's name to form Muhammad Ali Professional Sports, or MAPS, a promotional company. Smith was soon big in the fight game by spreading around large quantities of cash, sometimes delivered in pillowcases.

While people wondered where the money came from, nobody in the fight game really cared. The free ride came to an end, however, when Smith was arrested, and later convicted, on charges of embezzlement. The cash he had been generously spreading around came from Wells Fargo through an electronic heist. It turned out that Smith was actually Ross Fields, a small-time con man and check bouncer. Sentenced to ten years, Fields was out for the count.

Greg Who?

The heavyweight division has suffered since the departure of Muhammad Ali. Larry Holmes, for all his skill and accomplishments, simply never caught the public's eye the way ''The Greatest'' did. But after Holmes's departure, things went downhill even faster. Apart from the confusion and watering down resulting from three separate titles (WBS, WBC, IBF), there has been the problem of uninspired fighters. Among these was the most short-lived heavyweight champion. Greg Page gained the WBA title in December 1984 and lost it in April 1985, a dubious reign of 150 days.

The Fight We Didn't Need to See

If anybody needed another clue to the problems of the boxing world, the 1987 Spinks–Cooney bout was the answer. Billed as "The War at the Shore" in Atlantic City, the heavyweight confrontation matched Michael Spinks, a graduate from the light heavy division, against Gerry Cooney. Having lost a decision to Holmes some five years earlier, Cooney had added to his nearly extinguished career by defeating three nobodies in fights that totaled seven rounds. It was clear that if Cooney had been a black fighter, he would not be getting into the ring for the millions he was being guaranteed.

It was not a fight that captured the public's imagination. Instead of the "War at the Shore," it quickly became known as "The Bore on the Shore" and one boxing observer commented, "I have come to an absolutely definitive decision. They're both going to lose." It didn't turn out that way as Spinks dominated Cooney, presumably ending Cooney's boxing career. Until, that is, the next promoter looking for a white heavyweight contender comes along with enough loot.

The Fight We'd Like to See

After the Hagler–Leonard bout in 1987, archrivals Don King and Bob Arum scuffled in the audience, with King tossing in some choice anti-Semitic remarks and Arum making allegations of guns being carried by King's men. King challenged Arum to a fight. Why not? But please, do it the old-fashioned way. No gloves and fight to the finish.

Gorging George

He saw Ali do it. He saw Cooney do it. He saw Duran do it. He saw Leonard do it. So George Foreman, the onetime world heavyweight champ, decided he would also make a comeback. He did it in 1987, returning to the ranks of the heavyweights, with the emphasis on *heavy*. The thirty-eight-year-old Foreman, who had quit at 47–2 (his forty-two victories by knockout are the highest KO percentage of any heavyweight champ), returned to the ring at 269 pounds. That was 2 pounds more than Primo Carnera, the heaviest titleholder, was for his 1933 victory over Jack Sharkey. In case you missed it, Foreman won his return bout, but it didn't make any highlight films.

Still Foreman's poundage was mild compared with the greatest tonnage ever recorded in a boxing match. In 1971 Claude "Humphrey" McBride, who tilted the scales at 340 pounds, knocked out Jimmy Black, a dainty 360-pounder, in three rounds in Oklahoma City. Their combined 700 pounds of boxing fury are the most ever in the sport.

Professional Wrestling

By any rational definition, professional wrestling does not belong in a book about sports. But then this is a book about dubious sports. And nothing is more dubious than pro wrestling.

But Can Mick Jagger Deliver the Body Slam?

When the Rolling Stones played the New Orleans Superdome in December 1981, they drew 87,500 rock fans—the largest crowd to attend an indoor sporting or entertainment event. But in March 1987, Hulk Hogan and company eclipsed the sissy rock and rollers when Wrestlemania III, an all-star exhibition presented by the World Wrestling Frederation, pulled an awesome 93,173 wrestling aficionados—some paying as much as $100 per ticket—into Detroit's Silverdome.

It was a memorable night of wrestling. In the main event, WWF champion Hogan toppled the gargantuan Andre the Giant with a body slam and leg drop to retain his crown. In other matches, the Honky Tonk Man played a number on Jake "The Snake" Roberts; "The Dragon" Steamboat tamed Randy "Macho Man" Savage; and King Harley Race muzzled Junk Yard Dog. Hercules drew a disqualification. (How on earth does anybody get *disqualified* in professional wrestling?)

In tag team matches, Hillbilly Jim, The Haiti Kid and Little Beaver took the measure of King Kong Bundy, Little Tokyo and Lord Littlebrook, while Greg "The Hammer" Valentine and Brutus Beefcake sent Jacques and Raymond Rougeau packing. Need any more be said?

CHAPTER 7

Sports Miscellany: Olympics, Soccer, Golf and Other Weird and Wimpy Sports

Olympics

My Funny Valentin

Tokyo, 1964. Spanish featherweight Valentin Loren didn't know when to stop fighting. His Olympic outing turned out to be one referee's decision the fighter contested. During the second round of Loren's opening match, the young Spaniard was disqualified by Hungarian referee György Sermer because of repeated violations for holding and hitting with open gloves. Unhappy with that ruling, Loren took matters into his own hands. Literally. Closing his previously opened gloves, Loren delivered a haymaker— not to his opponent but to referee Sermer. His ill-aimed punch cost Loren more than the fight. He was banned from international amateur competition for life.

Loren wasn't the only unhappy boxer that year. When Korean flyweight Dong-Kih Choh was disqualified for holding his head too low, he staged a sit-down strike. For fifty-one minutes, the young boxer sat in the middle of the ring and refused to budge. Eventually he was persuaded to leave the ring. With all these boxing antics, the '64 Olypmics didn't need referees; they should have had a ringmaster!

Are You or Aren't Ewa?

Tokyo, 1964. The Polish women's team took the gold in a 4-by-100 meters relay, but their names were later removed from the Olympic record books. Ewa Klobukowsa, the Polish team's anchor, became the first athlete in Olympic history to flunk a sex test.

Of course that was in the days before compulsory sex education, so it's really no surprise that she didn't pass her exam.

Tamara, Tamara

In 1960 and 1964, Tamara Press of the Soviet Union overwhelmed her opponents in the shot put and discus. But when sex tests were ordered for international competition, Tamara and her sister Irina mysteriously disappeared from competition. You could say that's one way to stop the Presses.

Stella, Baby

Stanislawa Walasiewicz, better known as Stella Walsh, was a female track sensation of the 1930s. In Los Angeles in '32, running for the Polish team, she equaled the women's world record in the 100-meters, running with what one commentator called "long, man-like strides." Four years later, in Berlin, Walsh was upstaged by a young American sensation, Helen Stephens, who set a new world record in the event. Yet when she finished her racing career, Walsh had piled up eleven world records and two Olympic medals. In 1980 Walsh was the tragic innocent victim of a robbery and she was killed. Her autopsy undoubtedly shook up the medical examiner; Stella Walsh, he discovered, possessed male sex organs. Which goes a long way toward explaining those "man-like strides"!

No Wonder He Was Beamin'

Mexico City, 1968. It was a moment considered one of the most pure in sports history: Bob Beamon shattering the long-jump world record with a leap of 29 feet 2 inches—an improvement of almost 22 inches. The night before Beamon's great leap forward was anything but pure, however, and Beamon was not too sure he would be able to perform up to promised expectations. According to Dick Schaap's book *The Perfect Jump*, Beamon was involved in another sort of performance; for the first time in his career, Beamon made love on the night before a competition.

At the moment of orgasm, Beamon was overcome with the feeling that he had—to put it one way—"shot his wad," ruining any opportunity he might have had to deliver on the record he had boldly predicted.

In retrospect, his unorthodox pre-Games games look like a pretty good way to tune up.

Finnegan's Wake

Mexico City, 1968. Chris Finnegan was a twenty-four-year-old British bricklayer who went on to win the gold in boxing's middleweight division. But his toughest opponent would prove to be the specimen cup. As Finnegan himself later told it, "If there's one thing I've never been able to do, it's have a piss while someone's watching me. I can never stand at those long urinals you get in gents' bogs, with all the other blokes having a quick squint."

True to form, Finnegan came up empty even as onlookers and supporters whistled, turned on faucets and gave him four pints of beer to drink. Eventually he was allowed to go to dinner with two officials trailing along. Finally he jumped up and said, "Who wants some piss?" After passing water, Finnegan passed his most demanding test.

Standing on Ceremony

Mexico City, 1968–Munich, 1972. There's no question that the most notorious medal ceremony in Olympic history took place in Mexico City in '68. Tommie Smith and John Carlos, the 1–2 finishers in the 200-meter dash, stood barefoot and hung their heads while raising clenched, black-gloved fists as "The Star-Spangled Banner" was played. It was the athletes' symbol of black unity and was a protest against black poverty. The International Olympic Committee was not amused. The two were immediately suspended for making a political statement and given forty-eight hours to get out of town. (Smith went on to become track coach at Oberlin and later Santa Monica College; Carlos had a troubled post-Olympic career but got some measure of justice when he was hired as a consultant to the '84 Olympics in Los Angeles.)

In the wake of the Smith-Carlos performance, all eyes were on future sprinters and woe to anybody who failed to toe the line. In Munich four years later, Vince Mathews and Wayne Collett, the 1–2 finishers in the 400-meters, didn't do anything as ostentatious as their predecessors. They simply fidgeted and talked during the ritual anthem playing. A furious IOC banned the two from further competition. It must have worked. Nobody has tried it again!

When Wright Was Wrong

Munich, 1972. Eddie Hart and Rey Robinson were considered possible threats to Russian Varley Borzov in the glamorous 100-meter sprint which Borzov had dominated. After winning their heats, Hart, Robinson and Robert Taylor, a third U.S. sprinter, waited for the quarterfinals, which Coach Stan Wright had told them started at 7 P.M. But Wright had been working from a preliminary schedule that had been revised. As they watched on a television monitor in a network trailer, the three sprinters realized to their horror that they were supposed to be on the track. Taylor managed to make it to the track in time for his scheduled heat, but the other two men were eliminated without a chance to compete. About Coach Wright, Robinson later commented, "He can go on being a coach. What can I go on being?"

Half a Cup Is Better Than None

Munich, 1972. New Zealand's Rod Dixon, the surprise third-place finisher in the 1,500-meter run, was sobbing tears of joy after his Olympic dream came true. He should have saved his tears—he'd need the liquid. When he was taken for his drug test, Dixon could produce only a small sample. When he asked the official if it was enough, Dixon was told, "For the gold medal, no, but for the bronze, it will do."

Foiled: Whatever Became of Onischenko?

Montreal, 1976. Favored to take the fencing title, Soviet star Boris Onischenko wasn't leaving matters to skill or chance. He was using a rigged épée that falsely registered electronic hits. His British opponent, Jeremy Fox, protested that he hadn't been touched and officials quickly seized the suspicious weapon. Caught Red-handed, Onischenko was sent home, stripped of titles, given a menial job and later sent to Siberia. And what eventually happened to Boris? Curiously, he was discovered dead in his bathtub four years later. He had broken the cheater's cardinal rule: Do it, but don't get caught.

To the Victor, the Spoils

Moscow, 1980. An Olympic medal can often be the first step to riches, glory and fame. Just ask the Zimbabwean women's field hockey team. The American-led boycott of the '80 Games had the Soviets scrambling to fill some gaps in the competition. One lucky recipient was Zimbabwe (formerly white-ruled Rhodesia), which scraped together a women's field hockey team to be subsidized by the

Russians. The all-white Zimbabweans then caught the field by surprise and went on to win the gold. Their reward upon returning home? The minister of sport promised each player an ox!

Olympic Events We'd Like to See Again

Bring back the Tug-of-War. This event was a mainstay of the Summer Games between 1900 and 1920. In 1908 the event caused a scuffle when the American team, which lost in seconds to the British team—comprised of the Liverpool police—complained that the Brits had worn illegal boots with cleats, spikes and heels. The Liverpool police team said they were ordinary police boots, prompting the American team to withdraw from the event in protest.

The Games just haven't been the same since they canned this event.

Walk On By

"I knew something was wrong when I came to a locked gate."—U.S. race walker Ron Laird after going off the course in the Pan Am Games 20,000-meter walk.

Dear Old Dad

Lots of world-class athletes credit their parents with their success. All that nurturing and support while they were in training, you know. But nobody owes more to a parent than Mexican race walker Maria Colin. During the 1987 Pan Am Games in Indianapolis, Colin finished second behind countrywoman Graciela Mendoza. Lo and behold, Mendoza was disqualified for lifting her foot during the race, an infraction in race walking. Oh, by the way, among the three judges responsible for the disqualification was Pablo Colin, Maria's dear old dad. "They stole the medal from me," said an irate Mendoza. "It is his daughter. He wants her to win always." (For the record, all three judges had disqualified Mendoza.)

Thanks for the Help, Folks

With a few hundred yards to go, Great Britain's premier marathoner, James H. Peters, was winning the event in the 1954 Empire Games held in Vancouver. But as he entered the stadium, Peters began to weave and stagger. Ten times he fell only to rise and continue toward victory. All around him, spectators shouted encouragement, including, "That's what made England great." Finally Peters fell across what the spectators thought was the finish line and they picked him up and placed him on a stretcher. Moments later, a public address announcer informed the Good Samaritans that their help was premature— the finish line was on the other side of the track. Peters was disqualified. History fails to show how stiff he kept his upper lip upon hearing the news.

Be True to Your School

In a 1987 New York City public school championship, Tim McRae of Clinton High was disqualified from the long jump, his ouster costing his team the city title. The reason for his ouster from competition? He was not wearing school-issued shorts, which was against regulations. That'll teach you a good lesson, Tim.

Soccer

Roly-Poly Goalie

Soccer history shows that the largest goalie ever was England's Willie J. "Fatty" Foulke (1874–1916), who would authoritatively place his 6'3", 311-pound (later he weighed in at 364) frame in front of the goal. Fatty once stopped the action in a game when he snapped the goal's crossbar. The Fridge of his day, Fatty once ate the entire team's dinner before the rest of his teammates arrived.

A Great Bunch of Fans

Soccer fans around the world are always an interesting lot. Remember the war that began in South America after a controversial game? Lately, it has been the English soccer fans who have acquired a reputation that is most decidedly un-British. After the 1985 tragedy that took place in Brussels when a fight broke out between Liverpool and Italian fans resulting in 42 deaths and 400 injuries, British fans were banned from the Continent.

After the ban was lifted, one group of fans picked up where they left off. Traveling to Holland on a North Sea ferry for preseason exhibitions, British fans fought among themselves with knives and bottles. Three days later, Manchester fans in Amsterdam attacked a policewoman and trashed two restaurants and a tram. The fans were obviously in midseason form even though it was just the preseason.

Youth Will Be Served

Shouting "Kill the ref" is an ancient, time-honored tradition for fans who want to express their unhappiness with sporting officials. Some parents in Miami, Florida, wanted to take it literally. In the midst of a youth soccer league game in Boca Raton, fans (parents) of the Under-14 Miami Shores team harassed and abused the referee in the game for supposedly favoring the other team. With the score tied, the game moved to a shoot-out, but the ref ruled that the Shores players were offsides and the Shores fans went berserk, attacking the ref, leaving him bruised. He stopped the game and the Florida Youth Soccer Association suspended the Shores team until someone identified the assailant. So far, no one has.

Rough on Refs

Miami isn't the only tough place to work as a ref. In a 1987 game in Omaha, Nebraska, a teenage referee at an Under-9 game was beaten so severely by two mothers that he had to be hospitalized. And in New York, one soccer ref said: "I think the refs need to be protected. In a lot of places here we are scared with spectators on the sidelines. They have sticks, they have bottles and clubs."

Take That, You Bloody Fans

Maybe they were singing "Kill the Ref," too. But history does not record exactly what the fans of Glencraig United were chanting. It couldn't have been very polite. The referee took exception to the lyrics and "booked" all eleven players and two substitutes before the game even started.

Golf

In the words of sportswriter Westbrook Pegler, "Golf was, I should say offhand, the most useless outdoor game ever devised to waste the time and try the spirit of man." What is even sillier than playing, though, is watching golf on television. All that whispering could drive you crazy.

From Tee to Shining Tee

What a year Floyd Satterlee Rood had. You see, from September 14, 1963, to October 3, 1964, Floyd golfed his way across America as he played from the Pacific coast to the Atlantic coast. He shot 114,737, losing 3,511 balls along the 3,397.7-mile "course." History does not show how many divots he had to replace.

Throwing in the Towel

Craig Stadler must really love those fans. After Stadler finished the '87 Andy Williams Open in a three-way tie that should have earned him $37,333, he was ruled out of the money. Television viewers called the PGA and said that a film clip showed that Stadler had kneeled on a towel to play a shot from under a small tree. For the sin of "building a stance," Stadler should have assessed himself a two-shot penalty, but he didn't, making him guilty of signing an incorrect scorecard, an automatic disqualification. Picky, picky, picky.

Hole in 1(66)

Sometimes it just doesn't pay to get out of bed. An unnamed lady playing in a tournament in Shawnee-on-Delaware, Pennsylvania, hit a tee shot on the short 130-yard sixteenth. The ball carried into a river and floated. Setting out in a boat with her husband, she beached the ball a mile and a half downstream. One hundred sixty-six strokes later, after making her way through a forest, the determined lady sank that sucker.

Horse Before the Cart

High school senior Scott Frederick was disqualified after three holes of golf during the 1987 Kentucky state golf tournament. It seems that the youngster was riding a golf cart against regulations. It didn't even make a difference that Frederick was a 4'4" dwarf who was incapable of walking the course. Dwarfism, according to wise officials of the Kentucky State Athletic Association, does not count as a handicap. Makes you wonder who *really* has the handicap.

Toughest Course

Golfers the world over like to talk about the most difficult eighteen holes they have faced. But it takes a different sort of golfer to make it on the public links of New York City. According to *New York Times* reporter William Geist, urban golfers must contend with problems other than the usual sand and water traps. Typically the Fun City duffer must expect to hit out of abandoned subway cars, ward off muggers while putting and occasionally even pack a handgun in with the drivers. As the song says, "If I can make it there, I'll make it anywhere. . . ."

Weird World of Sports

Losers Shovel

For good, clean fun there's nothing like an elephant rodeo. And that's exactly what they do each year with 150 elephants at the Elephant Festival in Thailand. During the course of the three-day action, the elephants play soccer, roll logs and run sprints. The climax to each year's pachyderm Olympics is a tug-of-war that pits a single five-ton elephant against a team of 100 Thai soldiers.

Ralph Lauren, Eat Your Heart Out

Not yet sanctioned by the Thai Festival is elephant polo. First played in Jaipur, India, in 1976, polo on elephantback is growing in popularity. Clubs are springing up all over the place. The World Elephant Polo Association, formed in 1982, staged its first championships in 1983. Led by Captain Mark Payne, the Tiger Tops Tuskers took the prize.

My Old Ken-Ducky Home

Taking its cue from the Marx brothers movies *Duck Soup* and *A Day at the Races*, the town of Deming, New Mexico, each year becomes the Lexington, Kentucky, of the duck-racing world. In the recent annual duck races held there—where the course is known as "Duck Downs"—

the winner was Sunny, owned by a man named Robert Duck. The runner-up in the 400-duck field was entered by Bob's wife, Kathy Duck. The Ducks obviously take their ducks very seriously.

The Temptation Stakes

Leave it to San Francisco. When radio station KABL wanted to sponsor a St. Patrick's Day event as a station promotion, all the good ones were taken. So they made one up. Taking their cue from the legend that St. Patty had chased the snakes from Ireland, the station folks hit upon the notion of a St. Patrick's Day Snake Race. Since the first running in 1963, the event has become an annual tradition in Baghdad by the Bay. The snakes race along a series of eighteen-foot-long wooden troughs, the crown going to the snake that reaches the finish line first or travels farthest in three minutes. No boas or pythons, please.

Here's Mud in Your Eye

Frat boys will be frat boys. And sometimes that makes other people mad. Take the case of the Indians who picketed Santa Clara University in 1986. The Indians were enraged at reports that the Sigma Phi Epsilon–sponsored women's mud-wrestling contest were using dirt filched from sacred Indian burial sites. The company that delivered the dirt had reportedly told a local newspaper that the dirt had "come from the Indians." The dirt supplier recanted, saying they had only been joking. The vice president of the fraternity said, "I think we're going to stay away from mud wrestling for a little while."

Cleaning Up

Worlds away from the muck of mud wrestling is the sport that gives new meaning to the nautical phrase "old tub"—bathtub racing. Yes, each year up in Canada they run in Nanaimo–Vancouver World Championship Bathtub Race, the jewel in the crown of the Daily Free Press World Cup bathtub-racing circuit. Participants transform the family tubs into world-class cruisers by outfitting them with motors (spending as much as $3,600 in the process, some with corporate sponsorship). A silver-painted plunger goes to the first tubber to sink. Craig Bunch, winner of the 1986 race, won it, to put it one way, by running rings around the competition.

Something Fishy

Catch-and-release fishing competitions, especially those involving deep-sea fishing, are obviously difficult to police. So organizers usually rely on the honor system among the competitors. Officials trust the fishermen to radio in reports of their catches and then throw the fish back as a conservation measure. The competitors are kept honest by other entrants who fish in sight of each other. Recently, big tournaments have added another check system—mandatory polygraph tests for anyone in a cash-prize tournament. Supposedly, the lie detectors will keep the anglers from going crooked. The theory didn't stop somebody from trying. In a 1987 Billfish Tournament in Florida, three anglers aboard the *Playmate* reported enough catches to win the first prize of $4,500 and a trip to Costa Rica. Others in the contest became suspicious because the *Playmate* had been trolling and was often out of sight of others in the contest. Sure enough, the winners all flunked the test and were disqualified.

But Deltoids Are a Girl's Best Friend

In 1954, *Sports Illustrated* asked, "Do competitive sports tend to make women less feminine?"

"Well," came one response, "these women champions are very strong. I've always envied them their nice muscles. My husband smiles when I express my admiration for these women. Then he adds: 'Would a man rather take a lovely bit of femininity in his arms or a bundle of muscles?' I'm perplexed. I don't know." So spoke Marilyn DiMaggio, identified as a Hollywood movie star.

Horse Racing

Name Games

★ The New York–based Jockey club oversees the naming of thoroughbreds, and they do have some regulations. For instance, the use of commercial names is forbidden. So when U.S. Air came in a winner, the Club screamed "foul." Undaunted, the horse's owner rechristened the animal J.C. (for Jockey Club) Recall and the horse came in an 8–1 winner in its next race.

★ You have to like a horse named Cunning Stunt.

Laboring in the Stretch

Mary Bacon, one of the pioneer women jockeys, was riding in a race in 1969 only six days before giving birth.

Afterward she commented: "My mount that day was a mare in foal. I couldn't help but think about those fans betting on a pregnant horse ridden by a pregnant jockey. The four of us finished last."

Bowling

Surrender Dorothy

On January 24, 1926, Dorothy Meinecke of Detroit bowled 130 games in sixteen and a half hours—an average of 7.9 games per hour.

Bigger Balls

"One of the advantages of bowling over golf is that you very seldom lose a bowling ball."—Professional bowler Don Carter.

Marbles

Go, Toucans!

Talk about dynasties! Since the British Championship in marbles was established in 1926, the Toucan Terribles have taken all the you-know-whats a record twenty consecutive times (from 1956–75 they were unstoppable). In '71, the Terribles set the speed record by clearing the ring of forty-nine marbles in two minutes, fifty-seven seconds. Awesome!

Key Date in American History

January 13, 1957. The round plastic dish that would come to be known as the Frisbee is born to the Wham-O Manufacturing Corporation of San Gabriel, California. Rich Knerr, one of the former owners of Wham-O, says he named the disk after a newspaper cartoon character named Mr. Frisbie. (Wham-O also gave us the Hula Hoop, Super Ball and the slingshot whose distinctive "whammo" sound gave the company its name.)

CHAPTER 8

The Hall of Blame: Legendary Alibis and Excuses For Losing

The Hall of Blame is proudly dedicated to those great athletes throughout sports history who chose to look in any direction to find a reason for their failures. Any direction, that is, but their own. To each of the following Hall of Blamers goes an **"Ike,"** an award named in honor of the memorable Ring Lardner creation, **Alibi Ike,** a baseball player who could find an unusual excuse for any occasion.

Dropped Kicker

Before his Dallas Cowboy career ended in 1987 after his conviction on charges of sexual assault of a minor, placekicker Rafael Septien was among the National Football League's career leaders in weird excuses. To Septien, we award an **Ike** holding a sore toe for these beauties after blown kicks:

"I was too busy reading my stats on the scoreboard."

"The grass was too tall." (It so happened he was talking about the artificial surface of Texas Stadium.)

"My helmet was too tight and it was squeezing my brain."

What brain, Raffy?

A Screw Loes

Between 1950, when he broke in with Brooklyn, and 1961, when he retired, Billy Loes compiled a respectable 80–63 record with a 3.89 ERA. (He was less successful as a reliever with thirty-two saves and a 25–26 record.) Anything but respectable was his 1952 World Series performance against the Yankees. Pitching in game six with a 3–2 lead in games and ahead 1–0, Loes balked a runner to second and was facing opposing pitcher Vic Raschi. Raschi tapped one back to the mound which hit Loes in the knee and got by for an RBI single. An eighth-inning Mantle home run sealed the Yankee victory as the Dodgers lost the game 3–2 and the Series, four games to three. Afterward, Loes would make alibi history with this classic statement: "I lost it in the sun." To Loes, an Ike wearing designer shades.

How Do You Spell Relief? E-x-c-u-s-e

The 1986 National League Championship series had all the makings of a classic, with the Mets and Astros battling behind great pitching from both teams. But before long the two teams were also battling to get into the Hall of Blame with their finger-pointing after each loss. The Mets needed team-sized crying towels every time Mike Scott pitched. He devastated the New Yorkers, especially Gary Carter, with his split-fingered fastball, a pitch that the Mets claimed was a doctored ball.

The Astros were making their own bid for Blame-dom with their complaints that a bad call by first base ump Fred Brocklander had given the Mets a game.

But it took an epic sixth game in Houston to bring out a real Hall of Blame performance from Houston reliever Dave Smith. In three of their four victories in the League Championship Series, the Mets had come from behind to win. Astro reliever Charlie Kerfeld said, "They got to the pitchers in our bull pen. They did the job." Astro Manager Hal Lanier would only say, "Any time you have a three-run lead going into the ninth and lose, that has to be disturbing."

But Astro bullpen ace Smith would have none of it. "I'm not ashamed of our bullpen. Not at all. We didn't score the runs we needed. We should have scored more runs."

To Smith, an **Ike** with arms pointing in eight different directions.

The Team That Came in From the Cold

After a typically poor Knick first half in Philadelphia during the depressing 1986–87 season, several of the New Yorkers blamed their performance on the cold Spectrum floor. There must have been a lot of cold NBA floors that season as the Knicks went 24–58 on the season. To the 1986–87 New York Knicks, an **Ike** wearing a fur coat.

It's Not How You Lose, It's How You Leave the Game

Proving that excuses and poor sportsmanship are not the exclusive province of professionals, **The Hall of Blame** welcomes New Rochelle (New York) High School basketball coach Jim Bostic.

"We got raped. I really believe it. We were set up," said Bostic, explaining why he had pulled his team off the court with 1:27 remaining in overtime during a 1987 game. With rival Clarkstown South leading 58–55, Bostic yanked his team because, as he put it, "The way the officials handled the game was unconscionable. . . . They had fifteen fouls called on them, we had twenty-seven called on us. . . . It's not sour grapes. Something's going on."

In a touch of class, Bostic added, "There is no way that team could beat our team anywhere, anytime." To make sure of that, Bostic yanked his players and, in a classic Hall of Blame maneuver, blamed it on the officials. To Bostic, an **Ike** boarding a school bus—a yellow school bus, of course!

Tragic Arias

It's fairly typical to hear children scream, "You cheated," when they lose a game. But we expect a little more from the grown-ups, even if they are tennis players. Jimmy Arias wins a permanent place in **The Hall of Blame** for his petulant outburst after a loss to Andres Gomez in a 1987 tournament played in Brookline, Massachusetts.

The cries of foul play came after Gomez won a disputed third-set tie breaker. Arias hit a deep shot into the left corner and the lineswoman called it out. But then she reversed herself, saying the ball was good. Gomez spent the next fifteen minutes arguing, legitimately or not, that he had stopped going for the ball when he heard the out call. The point was ordered replayed. Gomez won it and the next three points as well to take the match.

Following the loss, a bitter Arias refused to shake hands with Gomez. "I was on a roll," said Arias. "Then we waited for twenty minutes and I lost all the momentum. . . . He just cheated, basically."

To Arias, a weeping **Ike** sucking its thumb.

Eat to Lose

It was probably the most shameful moment in modern boxing history. After a close match in Montreal in which Roberto ("Fists of Stone") Duran decisioned Sugar Ray Leonard, the two met again in 1980. Rather than going toe-to-toe with Duran as he had in their first fight, Leonard danced and shuffled, taunting a seemingly out of shape Duran. In the seventh, Leonard faked a "bolo" punch and suckered Duran with a left. Winded and stumbling, his heart obviously not in the fight, Duran clutched his stomach, held his gloves up in surrender and pleaded, *"No mas, no mas."* The boos of an angry crowd showering down on his head, Duran threw in the towel. To Duran, an **Ike** drinking Alka-Seltzer for his postfight claim that his stomach had cramped up because he had eaten too much steak and drunk too much orange juice prior to the match.

CHAPTER 9

**The Foul Plays Hall of Fame:
A Collection of the Flakes,
Freaks, Wackos and Other
Assorted Oddballs Who Have
Made Sports What They Are**

The Foul Plays Hall of Fame is dedicated to those sporting types who have made modern athletics what they are. These are the flakes and wackos of the playing fields, along with some of the more odious personalities in sport, who by dint of their special talent for doing the unexpected or, in some cases, totally alienating their fans, have carved themselves a special niche in sports history.

Owner's Box

As Hall of Famer Bill Terry put it, "Baseball must be a great game to survive the people who run it." And Terry never even had to play for any of these guys.

George Steinbrenner

In the good old days, baseball fans loved to hate the Yankees. As Red Smith put it, "It was like cheering for

U.S. Steel.'' From the days of Ruth and Gehrig through DiMaggio and up to the Mantle–Maris years, The Dynasty strung up pennant after pennant and accumulated its streak of World Series victories. But the Yanks fell on hard times in the late 1960s.

Then came Apocalypse in Pinstripes. In 1973 George Steinbrenner bought the team and people no longer had to hate the Yankees. Now they could hate the Yankees' owner.

His reign got off to an auspicious start when he pleaded guilty to making illegal contributions to the Nixon reelection campaign and was suspended by Commissioner Bowie Kuhn for two years, For players and fans, it wasn't long enough.

Here is the baseball genius who once told Ron Guidry, ''You'll never make it in this league.'' He is the classy individual who once told an NBC sports producer about to air a controversial Yankee tape, ''You better not play that tape on the air. I'm on the major league baseball television committee and NBC will get crapped all over.''

Perhaps Steinbrenner is best described by one of his former players, who anonymously called the Yankees owner ''a twenty-four carat asshole.'' Some other choice comments on the man they call ''The Boss'':

★ ''George Steinbrenner talks out of both sides of his wallet.''—Former ump Ron Luciano.

★ ''Steinbrenner has proved that you can buy social acceptance. If he weren't rich and powerful, who would even hang around with him?''—Author Art Hill.

★ ''I know how to tell when George Steinbrenner is lying—his lips move.''—Jerry Reinsdorf, White Sox co-owner.

★ "It would be helpful if George would go back to Cleveland and help wash his boats."—Former Yankee reliever Sparky Lyle.

★ "He has nothing to do with nothing."—Dave Winfield.

There is little doubt that George Steinbrenner's abrasive, boorish, impulsive, insulting behavior, and even worse, his uninformed baseball decisions, have cost the Yankees more fans than all the Yankee losses combined.

The last word on The Boss belongs to Don Baylor who escaped the mayhem of the Bronx and watched from afar as Steinbrenner hired Billy Martin for an unbelievable fifth term as manager. Said Baylor when asked if he ever wanted to lead the men in pinstripes, "No. I came into the game sane and I want to leave it sane."

Ted "Captain Outrageous" Turner

For all of his faults, Steinbrenner has not (yet) put on a uniform and sat in the dugout. Ted Turner had no such reluctance. In 1977, with the Atlanta Braves doing their best to look like the perennial cellar dwellers they are, Turner decided to take things into his own hands. After watching his team work up a sixteen-game string of losses, Turner sent Braves skipper Dave Bristol on a "coaching trip." Suiting up, Turner managed the team to a 3–2 loss, their seventeenth straight. NL President Chub Fenney said once is enough and cited a rule that managers could not hold an interest in the club. Turner was turned out.

★ Turner, on the losing streak: "This losing streak is bad for the fans, no doubt, but look at it this way. We're making a lot of people happy in other cities."

★ On another skid: "I'm sitting here and I've got a cocked pistol in my hand. Who can I give the Braves to in my last will and testament? I wish I was on Gilligan's Island. Everyone has so much fun there.'

★ Turner on himself: "If I only had a little humility, I would be perfect."

★ O's owner Edward Bennet Williams on Turner's free agent signing of Claudell Washington for $3.5 million: "Turner must be insane. This must be insanity."

★ "The man has mistaken his larynx for a megaphone." —Writer Steven Reddicliffe.

★ "He gets a good hold on the paintbrush, then confidently has the ladder removed."—Writer Roger Vaughan on Turner's approach to life.

★ In discussing his Goodwill Games, a mini-Olympics staged in Moscow and shown on Turner's TBS Superstation, Turner commented on his new role as ambassador without portfolio;: "I want to be like Jiminy Cricket for America—its conscience."

With Ted Turner for a conscience, we're in big trouble.

Calvin Griffith

In case you were wondering what caused the breath of fresh air in baseball, it was probably the departure of Calvin Griffith as lord and owner of the Minnesota Twins, the last bastion of plantation life in the big leagues. Remember what the tightfisted, mean-spirited Griffith said when he moved his franchise to Minnesota?

"I'll tell you why we came to Minnesota. It was when I found out you only had 15,000 blacks here. Black people don't go to ball games, but they'll fill up a wrassling ring and put up such a chant it'll scare you to death. . . . We came here because you've got good, hardworking white people here."

Of Griffith, pitcher Bill Lee said, "Everyone who plays for Griffith hustles like crazy so that some other club will make a trade and get the player away from Griffith."

Robert Irsay

The headlines could have read, "Dolt Bolts, Steals Colts."

It was in the quiet hours of March 29, 1984. Like a thief in the night, the owner of the Baltimore Colts had fifteen Mayflower moving vans, borrowed from Mayflower's owner at the request of Indianapolis Mayor Hudnut, sneak into the Colts' training facility and "steal" the team—jockstrap and barrel—under the cover of darkness. Transplanted to the Hoosier Dome in "India-no-place," the Colts became the sad sacks of the NFL. While sorry to see the team go, Baltimore fans were probably happy to see the backside of Robert Irsay.

Irsay's irationality in football matters has been devastating.

★ 1974: He ordered coach Howard Schnellenberger to replace quarterback Marty Domres with the inexperienced Bert Jones. The coach refused and Irsay marched down to confront Schnellenberger, who told Irsay to leave the field. That was the end of Schnellenberger's Colt career.

★ 1981: Irsay called Coach Mike McCormack from his box and told him to alternate quarterbacks on every play and call only pass plays—he wanted to show a friend in his box a touchdown. McCormack agreed. Later that year, Irsay started calling plays from the owner's box on a regular basis.

★ 1983: Unable to sign John Elway as their first-round choice, Irsay traded the quarterback away for two players and a 1984 first-round pick—without telling his coach, Frank Kush. (The pick was used to select guard Ron Solt.)

★ 1987: Just when you thought Irsay couldn't sink any lower, he did. Irsay announced that he would not pay fullback Randy McMillan his salary while he recuperated from an auto accident. "I'll talk to him if he gets well," said Irsay, "but if he doesn't, I don't even want him at our training complex."

Broadcast Booth

Howard Cosell

As Mr. Tell It Like It Is put it himself in typically pompous redundancy, "Let us reflect back nostalgically on the past." For years the insufferable Cosell pontificated about sports, thinking himself some modern-day Homer describing the Trojan Wars. Most of the time he sounded like an overinflated bag of wind whose highfalutin vocabulary was a veiled insult to listeners—Cosell's smug, superior on-air tone always sounded as if he thought no one else understood what he was saying. The truth of the matter is that few really cared what he was saying.

After years of pumping up boxing, Cosell turned on it

and now wonders why the business has turned rotten—oblivious to the fact that his shilling helped create the monster. The same applies to football. After helping create the myth of Monday Night Football, Cosell retired and started asking probing questions about why the Super Bowl and other football contests get so much "hype." After he left ABC's Monday Night Football and Baseball telecasts, viewers all over America felt it was safe to turn the sound back on. On Cosell:

★ "More than anyone I know, he sucks the oxygen out of a room."—Writer David Halberstam.

★ "I see where Anwar Sadat has kicked ABC out of Cairo. Most people just turn down the sound when Cosell is on."—Sportswriter Dick Young.

★ "If Howard Cosell was a sport, it would be Roller Derby."—Sportswriter Jimmy Cannon.

★ On his own work: "There are two professions that one can be hired at with little experience. One is prostitution. The other is sportscasting. Too frequently, they become the same."

★ "I tell it like it is. Howard Cosell tells it like Roone Arledge wants it told."—Sportscaster Harry Caray.

★ "He changed his name from Cohen to Cosell, put on a toupee and 'tells it like it is.' "—Sportswriter Jimmy Cannon.

★ The last word goes to boxing promoter Irving Rudd, commenting on the statement that Howard Cosell is his own worst enemy: "Not while I'm alive."

Coach's Room

Woody Hayes

When he died in 1987 at the age of seventy-four, it seemed that all of his victories (205–61–10 at Ohio State) were secondary to the devastating moment that finished his career. He punched out sportswriters, swung at TV cameramen and smashed down markers. But the image that will go down in sports history is Hayes on the sidelines of the 1978 Gator Bowl. His team trailing, Hayes became enraged when an Ohio State pass was picked off by Clemson linebaker Charlie Bauman. Hayes grabbed Bauman by the neck and punched at his helmet. In retrospect, it was a pathetic moment—a dinosaur struggling against the future. On Hayes:

★ "Woody was consistent. Graceless in victory and graceless in defeat."—Sportswriter Jim Murray.

★ Big Ten Commissioner Wayne Duke had a slightly different view: "Woody reminds me of Churchill's description of Montgomery: Indomitable in defeat, insufferable in victory."

Bobby Knight

The Woody Hayes of college basketball, Knight prompts two questions. How long before he ends up like Hayes, and why does the NCAA and Indiana University tolerate his behavior? The answer to the second question has to do with Knight's winning ways. His obnoxious antics will be permitted as long as he puts fannies in the Hoosier bleachers. About the first question, if a seat tossed across the court—resulting in a modest suspension—doesn't finish him, what will?

Typical of NCAA treatment of Knight is the fine leveled against him after the 1987 tournament which his Indiana team won. In an ugly display of his distemper, Knight banged on the scorer's table. It was an undisguised attempt to intimidate the officials, and for all we know it may have worked. Knight's fine: $10,000, to be deducted from Indiana's winning purse of more than $1 million!

Knight's lowest point, of course, came during the 1979 Pan Am Games when he was coaching the American team in Puerto Rico. In an altercation with a local policeman, Knight allegedly called the man a "nigger" and punched him. Skipping out on his court date, Knight was convicted in absentia. Unrepentant to the last, Knight later told an audience in Indiana that on the plane ride home from Puerto Rico, he "unzipped my pants, lowered my shorts and pressed my bare ass on the window. That's the last thing I wanted those people to see of me." A Puerto Rican journalist was in the audience and recorded the remarks, which got a big laugh in Knight's home court.

But Puerto Ricans may yet get the last laugh. A 1987 Supreme Court decision may have opened the way for Puerto Rico to attempt to extradite Knight to serve out his six-month sentence.

Biters, Brawlers and Bad Boys

Dick Butkus

All those Lite beer commercials have helped rehabilitate

the former Bear linebacker's image. But the players on the other side of the line of scrimmage have little trouble remembering Butkus as the dirtiest and most violent player on the gridiron. After viewing films of Butkus in action, current Bear Doug Plank commented, "He was unbelievable. I love to see—and listen—to him play. When he's going after somebody, Butkus sounds like a lion chewing on a big piece of meat."

Chew he did. No one was safe from the ferocious linebacker's teeth, even officials. In a 1969 exhibition, referee Ralph Morcroft was pulling Butkis off a pileup and Butkus responded by biting the official's finger to the bone.

On Butkus:

★ "Butkus just grabbed the lower part of my leg and tried to crack it in half over his knee. It was like you'd break up kindling for a fire. He didn't break it. I guess my leg was too green."—Green Bay running back MacArthur Lane.

★ "He doesn't want to hurt you. He wants to kill you." —Running back O. J. Simpson.

Brian Bosworth

The All-American linebacker from Oklahoma may yet become the most foul thing to hit pro football since Dick Butkus bit his last running back. With his orange Mohawk haircut and number 44 and "Boz" earrings, The Boz is sure to ruffle some NFL feathers. Banned from the Orange Bowl when he tested positive for steroid use, Bosworth was also not welcome to return to Coach Barry Switzer's Sooner team even though he had a year of eligibility left. The Boz then announced he would skip the regular college draft and opt for a supplemental draft held in June, 1987. Picked by the Seahawks, Bosworth pledged he wouldn't sign with the team. In August, he gritted his teeth and managed to swallow an $11-million, ten-year-contract package, giving the untried rookie the most lucrative contract for an NFL defensive player. Money talks!

What kind of stand-up guy is this All-American? Why, he's just the sort of hero that every father wants his son to emulate.

★ 1986: The Boz tells *Sports Illustrated* that when he worked summers at a GM auto plant, co-workers taught him how to sabotage cars. Every so often, out of boredom, somebody would hang a screw or bolt on a piece of thread inside the framework, just to drive the future owner mad. Said the Boz, "If you own a Celebrity or Century made in 1985 in Oklahoma city, that car is ——— if I had anything to do with it."

★ On his playing style: "I like to spit a loogie in a guy's face after I tackle him."

★ On quarterbacks: I hate unathletic-looking quarterbacks the most. Like Elway. He's knock-kneed. He has a big rear. And that awful-looking large mouth."

Marvin "Bad News" Barnes

For professional basketball, no news really is good news. Rarely has so much basketball talent been squandered as in the case of Barnes. A star with Providence College, Marvin Barnes had already acquired a "rep" for his high school antics. He once joined some kids who stole money from a bus driver. The problem was that Barnes was wearing his varsity jacket—the school's name was in prominent letters on the back and on the front was inscribed "Marvin." Good move, News.

In 1974 Barnes was given probation for assault on a Providence teammate with a tire iron. He violated that probation when he went through a Detroit airport metal detector with a gun in his gym bag. When asked why he had earned so many credits while in prison, Barnes replied, "There was no place I could go to cut classes."

Even after leaving the NBA, Barnes caused problems for teammates. The New Jersey Nets were banned from the L.A. Marriott because Barnes had skipped out on $1,600 in charges incurred during a previous team stay there.

John McEnroe

When on top of his game, there's no one better with a tennis racket. But all too often,the biggest part of his game was and is his vile temper, petulant antics and constant whining and bullying of officials. Tagged "McNasty" by the British tabloids that take delight in goading him, McEnroe quickly surpassed both Ilie Nastase and Jimmy Connors, tennis's first generation of beasty boys. A McEnroe sampler on officials and opponents:

★ To Wimbledon ump Edward James: "You are the pits of the world."

★ To a turbaned Kenyan linesman during a doubles match against the Armritraj brothers: "You're Indian. You're biased."

★ To a linesman at the French Open: "You French frog fag."

★ To Czech Tomas Smid, who sent a ball straight at McEnroe: "You'll be sorry the day you hit me, you f——g Communist asshole."

★ During Davis Cup play in 1987 against Boris Becker of West Germany, Mac became annoyed when the match grew long and many fans departed in search of something to eat. His mood worsened as the American crowd seemed to favor Becker. McEnroe commented: "Let them get some sauerkraut on their hot dogs."

With his track record of verbal abuse, McEnroe is certainly a likely candidate for stiff penalties, and that's just what he got after a four-letter tirade during the '87 U.S. Open: suspended from the Grand Prix circuit for two months. But, as it turns out, it's not such a tough life after all. Mac couldn't compete in several tournaments, all offering prizes of around $40,000. Instead he had to settle for an appearance in an eight-man exhibition match, which he won. His paycheck at this substitute event: $150,000. With "punishments" like that, it seems that more players will be looking for trouble in the future.

Left Fielders

Charlie Kerfeld

Call him the Astro-nut. In 1986 he was a sensation in the Houston bullpen—until the playoffs and the Mets came around. But his punk haircut and wild statements seem to suit a California or East Coast team more than the staid wastelands of Texas.

He calls himself "The Pterodactyl," explaining that his job as set-up man is to come out of the bullpen and "*swarp* down on them until it's time to get a save and let 'The Vulture' [ace Dave Smith] finish them off."

During the '86 season when Kerfeld was stingy with the runs, he wore a "Jetsons" T-shirt under his uniform. In the one appearance in which he forgot to wear the T-shirt, he allowed two unearned runs.

The presence of the inimitable Yogi Berra on the Astros bench as a coach seems to have rubbed off on the reliever. Kerfeldisms have come to have as much color—and make as much sense—as some classic "Yogiisms." A Kerfeld sampler:

★ Speaking of the pitching staff: "Jim Deshaies was a good accusation."

★ During the '86 campaign: "It's our season of destination."

★ On his off-day activities: "I go out and do what we call slam-dancing—go out and butt our heads and stuff like that."

A brief 1987 holdout, Kerfeld eventually signed for $110,037.37 and thirty-seven boxes of orange Jell-O. Yes, his uniform number is 37.

In the era of pitchers who sand, scuff and smear, who knows what a little orange Jell-O might do to a baseball!

Jim McMahon

There's no question about it. Jim McMahon is an original. Mike Ditka certainly must have known something was up when his first-round draft pick, the record-setting BYU quarterback, showed up for camp holding a can of beer as he stepped out of his limo. When Ditka issued a dress code for road trips requiring the Bears to wear shirts with collars, McMahon dazzled the football fashion world in a backless T-shirt with a priest's collar tied around his neck. He has also been known to play golf with spikes on the bottom of his sandals.

No doubt Ditka considers his number-one quarterback a pain in the ass. But in McMahon's case, that's literally the truth. McMahon displayed his best side during the 1986 Super Bowl pregame hype in New Orleans. Troubled by pain in his buttocks, Jimmy Mac had brought along his personal acupuncturist—inciting another small squall because the Bears refused to pay the guy's planefare. Wearing one of his patented headbands that read ACUPUNCTURE and surrounded by a massed media, McMahon noticed a helicopter above the field. Figuring the world wanted to know exactly where the pain was, Mac ''dropped trou'' and his aching derriere was prominently displayed on sports pages across America.

Ditka, who has his own view of Mac-Mayhem, offers the last word on his star QB: ''The shoulder surgery was a success. The lobotomy failed.''

Bill Lee

When Gary Hart took a breather from the 1988 presidential campaign, it looked pretty dull until Bill Lee came along. Remember the one and only ''Spaceman''? He was the wild-bearded left-hander for Boston and Montreal who got into hot syrup with Bowie Kuhn when he told reporters that he sprinkled marijuana on his pancakes.

In 1987 Lee was pitching himself as a candidate for President from the Rhinoceros Party, the U.S. offshoot of an irreverent Canadian group that proposes such things as abolishing the law of gravity. As part of his shaky platform, Lee wanted to abolish guns and butter. "They both can kill you," said Lee. He was also in favor of "Star Wars." "It wasn't a bad movie," said Lee in launching his own starry-eyed campaign. More from outer space:

★ "Baseball is a lot like the army—there aren't many individuals. About the only difference is that baseball players get to stay in nice hotels instead of barracks."

★ "If I were a Tibetan priest and ate everything perfect, maybe I'd live to 105. The way I'm going now, I'll probably only make it to 102. I'll give away three years to beer."

★ "I believe you come back as whatever you abused in the previous life. If you're a dope smoker, you might come back as a tree and get processed into Zig-Zag. . . . I hope to come back as a grain in the field and get turned into some of the finest Dortmunder Union beer in Germany. And that Pele will drink me."

★ "A 'flake' is a term created by a right-handed, egotistic, consumeristic, exploitative, nonrecycling, carnivorous, right-handed—I've said that, haven't I—population. You get the gist. It couldn't have been a term created by a left-hander."

More
Fun & Games from
WARNER BOOKS